P9-BEE-935

What people are saying about *#FeelFreeToLaugh*

"*#FeelFreeToLaugh* might be the most profound, impactful book I have read in my 90+ years on this earth. On the other hand, it might not be. I wouldn't know because I'm still trying to interpret the title. Also, can someone tell me what a hashtag is?"

The Reverend Billy Graham

"Jordan Baker Watts entertains and warms the heart with her debut literary work, *#FeelFreeToLaugh*. She also raises awareness about one of today's most pressing issues—the muffin top. She provides readers with ample reasons to invest in multiple pairs of Spanx, and for that I'm eternally grateful."

Sara Blakely
Founder, Spanx

"We are big fans of Jordan's writing, and we are proud to endorse *#FeelFreeToLaugh*. Jordan's heart and love for God shine brightly through her words, and she offers hope for weary moms everywhere. Also, her children (whom she writes about often) are wonderful. So cute. Beautiful, really. Their intelligence is unparalleled; they're definitely destined for greatness. Did we mention that they're absolutely adorable? Not that they're cuter than anyone else's grandchildren, but…ahhhh, nah, of course they are."

Bill and Lindsay Baker
Jordan Baker Watts's parents

"Jordan's openness and vulnerability are apparent throughout the pages of *#FeelFreeToLaugh*. She's real and raw and she doesn't hide away the messy parts of her life. Or mine. I mean, for real, Babe, did you have to talk about my abundance of back hair?"

Brandon Watts
Jordan's husband

#FeelFreeToLaugh

#FeelFreeToLaugh

Laughter and Lessons From Motherhood
(and stories to make you feel better about yourself)

Jordan Baker Watts

#FeelFreeToLaugh

All rights reserved. Except for brief excerpts for review purposes, no part of this book may be reproduced or used in any form without written permission from the publisher.

The people and products mentioned in this book are for illustration purposes only. Their mention is not intended in any way to imply or be an endorsement on the part of the publisher, nor do we vouch for them or their quality.

All Scripture quotations, unless otherwise noted, are taken from the ESV.

Cover Art and Design by Square 8 Studio
www.square8studio.com // @square8studio

Copyright © 2016 Jordan Baker Watts
All rights reserved.
ISBN-13: 9781537307206
ISBN-10: 1537307207
Library of Congress Control Number: 2016914228
CreateSpace Independent Publishing Platform
North Charleston, South Carolina

Dedication

To my for-life girls…you know who you are. You've cried with me. You've laughed with me. You've laughed AT me. You've done life with me. You've loved me without reserve and you've accepted me fully for as long as I can remember. There's never been a moment when I haven't felt safe with you, and there's never been a second that I've doubted your love for me. Friendships like ours don't come around too often, and ours is truly one for the books. From Lions to Eagles to wives and now mothers, it's my joy to walk through life with you. I love you forever and am eternally better for knowing you.

Contents

Acknowledgments

Special thanks to Lindsay Baker for her countless hours of editing, listening, and encouraging, and for teaching me everything I know about motherhood. Thanks to my kids for allowing me time away to work on this literary ~~masterpiece~~ and for providing me with an abundance of material to pull from. Thanks to my husband for choosing me all those years ago and for still choosing me today. I'm so grateful to do this life with you, and I'm grateful that you allow me to be real and raw in my writing about our family, even when it's less than flattering. I'm proud of the hot mess we call our family, and I adore you, back hair and all! Also, thanks for always telling me my legs are hot, even though they're plagued with cellulite. You're a #keeper.

Introduction

Don't Hate Me, But I'm Taking a Cruise

Well, hello! I didn't see you sitting there. I mean that literally, because it's physically impossible for me to see you as I sit here typing this introduction. Get it? (Let's pause for a moment to listen to the crickets.)

I know what you're thinking right now: "Oh, great, I'm one sentence into this book and already I can tell that this chick is not funny." But I beg you, give it time. I like to start a little slow on the uptake so as to make it an extra-fun surprise when I actually present material that's humorous. It is scientifically proven to elicit twice the laughs. Seriously. Look it up on Wikipedia, because the internet is never wrong.

#StayOffWebMD

Let me tell you a little about myself. I'm Jordan. I'm Brandon's wife and a mom to Emerson, Sutton, and Foster. I am a musician by trade and a Bond Girl in my dreams. I love carbohydrates, brownies (I consider brownies to be in a class of their own, apart from carbs), red wine, and Jimmy Fallon. And I'm currently sitting on a navy blue semi-comfortable chair in the middle of a cruise ship terminal waiting to board a massive boat. Yes, I am going on a cruise.

Alone.

#MomWin

When I checked in with the cruise line at the Miami airport, the first question the lady asked me was, "Are you traveling alone?" To which I replied, "HECK, YES, I'M TRAVELING ALONE!"

I'm still not sure whether the strange look she gave me was because I am cruising solo, because I seemed like I was excited about cruising solo, or because I still had the indentions of the airplane window shade mashed across the right side of my face. (I napped like a boss on the flight down to Miami.) #Zzzzzzzzz

Back to the cruise. Yes, I'm taking one. And I'm taking one all by myself (like a big girl or like a creepy cat lady; I'm not sure yet which one I am). My goals for this trip are, in no specific order, to: sleep a lot, eat a lot, sleep a lot, maybe walk the track a few times so I don't feel completely and utterly gross, sleep a lot, and write a book.

Yeah, there's the whole writing-a-book thing. That's sort of the reason I'm taking this voyage, hence me currently working on my laptop in the cruise ship terminal. I have to be honest with you: I have really questioned whether or not I am supposed to write this ~~epic~~ piece of literature. God already tells us in Scripture that the Word contains all the truth we need to know Him and to walk through life with wisdom and godliness. In a world with enough self-help books to, lined end to end, wrap around the earth's circumference 124 times, why add a book of my own to the mix? (Before any of you jump back on Wikipedia to correct me, yes, I totally made that earth-wrapped-in-books stat up, so save it.)

After much prayer and reflection, I feel like the Lord showed me clearly why I am to put pen to paper for ~~my mom~~ you to read. It's not that I'm writing about anything new (after all, there's nothing new under the sun), presenting some profound idea to you that can't be found in God's Word. I am, though, writing about these timeless truths from a perspective that the apostle Paul probably never had (read: frenzied mom of three). I'm simply taking the truths found in Scripture and repackaging them to directly relate to women and moms in the twenty-first century. Also, I will be tying in a lot of embarrassing stories about potty training and waxes gone wrong, so there's that.

#PoopIsFunnyNoMatterHowOldYouAre

In case you slept through the reading of the front cover, the title of this book is *#FeelFreeToLaugh*. It could alternately be titled *#MyLife* or

#TheseThingsAlwaysHappenToMe. You know you have a crazy life and bizarre experiences when people call you and say things like, "I had a total Jordan Watts experience today!"

Ummm…thanks?

#MyCrossToBear

I would wager a guess that everyone reading this book right now falls into one or both of the following groups: those who have moms and those who are moms. It's my hope that you'll enjoy this book no matter which group you belong to. Motherhood is amazing, there's no doubt about it. It's hard. It's exhilarating. It's tiring. It's humbling. It's infuriating. It's funny.

In my experience as a mom of three, there are plenty of situations that bring me to my knees, and I often have the choice to either laugh or cry about them. I have found over the years—although I often have to relearn this simple truth—that when I choose laughter, my load is lightened and my heart is renewed. It also infuriates my kids, which can be an added benefit.

The Lord knows that being a mom is hard. He is near, to be sure, to the worn and broken mothers who haven't laughed in as long as they can remember, and He is the God of all comfort. However, I have found that when I choose laughter over tears, He is also the Giver of an unexplainable joy. He is all about restoration, and I have seen time and again the ways He restores to me the joy that is mine in Him. If He can do it for me after some of the stories you will read about in the pages to come, rest assured, He can do it for you, too!

My heart's desire is to encourage you, whether you're a road-weary mother who can't find it in her to laugh, or a foster parent who gives of herself all day, every day, and needs to be filled up, or maybe, as is often true but rarely spoken about, you aren't a mom (yet). Your heart may ache with a deep longing to start a family, but it's not happening for you. Maybe you're exhausted, Single Mom, and you don't have time to brush your teeth at night, let alone laugh. Let me be the first to say clearly: I don't have all the answers, but my heart is to encourage you and to hopefully fill you up with the hope and love of Christ.

Along with laughter, you will quickly find that I am all about REAL. Maybe you're like me and you've found that the older you get, the harder it becomes to put on a façade of perfection. For instance, my driver's license says I weigh 140 pounds. The older I get, the more apparent it is that I do not, in fact, weigh 140 pounds. Subsequently, I must ask: at what point is it no longer acceptable for a woman to refer to her "baby weight" as "baby weight?" My baby just turned five. Can I call it "mid-size human weight," maybe? It sounds a lot more politically correct than "brownie weight."

#JustSaying

Maybe you're desperate for real. Real friendships. Real successes. Real failures. Real dreams. Real fears. In our current culture, the pressure to appear like we've got it all together in life feels suffocating (at least to me).

#CannotDeal

I see moms who are put together and organized and disciplined and marathon runners and Pinterest-y and PTA-President-y and I start to twitch nervously. I'm that mom in carpool who's wearing the yoga pants that have a hole in the seam along my rear end that I haven't noticed yet (yes, this actually happened), the one who has yesterday's mascara smeared under my eyes because I haven't had time to wash my face yet. I'm probably chewing gum because my breath smells, and my minivan looks like a chicken-nugget-and-goldfish bomb exploded inside, as noted by the preschool teacher who used to open the van door for my boys. But, like it or not, that's me (a solid four out of seven days each week). And I am at the point in my life and in my walk with God where I am okay with it. Do I want to be more disciplined? Yes. Do I want to have a clean van? Without a doubt. Do I want to be put together sometimes, to feel pretty and presentable and less…errr…fluffy? Of course I do. Do I want to run a marathon? This one is questionable.

#WillRunForFood

The myth that many women believe is that if we cannot present ourselves as perfect, we are somehow worthless. Expired, even. Past our prime. Well, hear me clearly, girls: if you've bought into this idea before, know right now that it's a lie from the pit of hell! It's time for us as women to champion each other, to be women who come as they are and not as they should be. I want to share my struggles without being looked upon with disdain. I want to say what I am really feeling and not what I think someone else wants to hear, all while knowing I'll be listened to with compassion and understanding. I want to dream big dreams and not be looked upon as a girl who just hasn't grown up yet. I want to be ME!

And I want you to feel comfortable being YOU. To take some time to rest in your own skin and to see that it's actually very lovely skin to be in. To pay attention to how comfortably it fits you, like it was made just for you, because it was, in fact, made just for you. And I want you to never look back.

Can we make a commitment to each other right now to set aside the masks we often wear, at least for the time that we are bound together by the words written on the pages of this book? As I sit here writing, I want you to know that I am making that commitment to you, too. I am going to pour out my honest heart, to share things about myself that might not be flattering, to be vulnerable enough to show the ugly parts of myself to you, and to dream out loud on the pages to come. And maybe, just maybe, we can begin to build an army of women who walk in freedom, women who fully own the people God made us to be. People like us, they're out there, I promise. We just have to look for them.

So, to recap: my goal in writing *#FeelFreeToLaugh* is to give you an excuse to laugh, and to share in a real way about my journey through motherhood and womanhood so far. And, just a reminder: there's lots of poop talk. If a book like that sounds like Chinese water torture to you, I would suggest you go ahead and put this one down carefully and back away slowly. Then just pass your copy of *#FeelFreeToLaugh* along to your funny friend—you know the one—because she'll like it. I promise.

#FunnyPeopleGetIt

I

Me

"Allow myself to introduce...myself."

—*His Grooviness, Austin Powers*

Childhood (The Mini-Michael-Bolton Years)

I believe it's been said that one's past should never define one's future, or something sage like that. Well, let me be the first to shout out an amen and a hallelujah, because if my past defined me now I'd still look like this:

No, that's not a #TBT picture of Michael Bolton at age eight. It's me, in all of my frizzy and fro-tastic glory. The white turtleneck serves to highlight my curly mullet and severe overbite so well. The only thing that could have made me look any cuter would have been if I had worn my neon-green headgear, but ~~un~~fortunately I think I was in between sets of braces at that moment so the headgear was not an option. Seriously, life was not very kind to me in those days.

I was born with a big, brown, curly mop of hair that my very-blonde-and-straight-haired mother tried to tame until my teenage years. I can't blame her ~~too much~~ (honestly, she didn't know better) but the whole hair sitch was no bueno. Her first mistake: she brushed my dry, curly hair. Even as I type this, I know that everyone with curly hair just gasped and cried silent tears for me as they understand the problem with this immediately: you never, EVER, under ANY circumstance, brush curly hair when it's dry. It's the cardinal sin of she-who-bears-ringlets. Brushing dry curls basically breaks the larger, softer curl into a million little tiny curls, thus eliminating the silky ringlets and creating a frizz nest large enough for a bald eagle to incubate its eggs in. My mother also apparently had never heard of hair gel, which didn't help the frizz issues.

#ThanksMom

Around age ten, I discovered that I had a very awesome talent: I could grow my fingernails out super-long. And grow them, I did. I was pretty sure people thought I was fabulous because I had very luxurious nails. Now I know that I was just a creepy ten-year-old with witch hands. They were usually painted bright red, and each paw usually sported at least one short nail because of the inevitable breakage.

#Klassy

What else can I say to accurately depict my early childhood? Well, I was homeschooled (not a knock on homeschooling, just a fact), my best friend's and my favorite thing to do was pretend that we were hamsters (speaking of which, it's your turn to build us a nest, Heather), and I liked to sew bonnets for my American Girl doll on my friend Mary Beth Doozan's sewing machine. Yes, you read that correctly. Bonnets. To match her bloomers and aprons.

#IWasTheCoolest
#IShouldHaveMadeHerAmericanGirlHeadgear

As the years progressed and I matured both physically and emotionally, things did not get much better. I struggled with severe insecurity. When I started my period and wore D-cup bras at age eleven, needless to say I felt awkward and unsure of myself. Those feelings carried over into middle and high school, and my insecurities defined me. I wasn't cute and tiny, sporting a size extra-small body like my friends. I wasn't conventionally pretty with my big head of curly hair and my second set of braces. I tried to focus on the things I was good at, like music and soccer, but I was racked with self-doubt and self-hatred. I know this sounds like a sad story in what's supposed to be a funny book, so let me say this, long story short: God ultimately brought me great healing and freedom, and I am now able to laugh about my awkward childhood because I know that it in no way defines me. And because a lot of it really is funny and I have since discovered hair gel.

#TakeThatMichaelBolton

Me Now (I'm THAT Lady)

Let's fast-forward to today. I am THAT lady. You know the one; you've seen her before. The mom who remembers ten minutes before a birthday party that we don't have a gift for the birthday kid. The one who runs into Target and grabs a clearance item that doesn't look too cheap but is, in reality, very cheap, hence the red clearance tag that I have to scrape off with my (still) chipped fingernails as I drive to the party. I arrive five minutes late and only remember in that very moment that I forgot something sort of essential at the store: gift wrap. Full disclosure: I actually dropped my daughter off at a birthday party recently with a gift that was "wrapped" in a plastic Target bag. You need to understand that in Atlanta, Georgia, especially in the affluent suburb in which we live, this is a cardinal mom-sin. I had to scrape a few jaws off the floor when I walked in carrying that gem of a gift. That said, I'm really okay with it, because I know that in a world of curly ribbons and handmade gift tags, I'm a plastic Target bag. I'm plain and simple, but I get the job done. Ish.

I'm the mom who arrives to drop my son off at preschool (late, naturally), only to realize as I enter his classroom that it's pajama day. Does my son have on pajamas? That would be a negative. Who knew that wearing play clothes to school could be so traumatic for a four-year-old? His teacher assured me it was on the calendar. And it was. It was on the calendar that had been used in my car as a weapon to smash a large black ant and then ended up in a wrinkled ball underneath the passenger seat...

...of my minivan. I'm the mom who drives a minivan. Not a cool minivan with a DVD player and gaming system and a touch-screen GPS. Nope, ours is old, it's geriatric blue, and it has a huge dent on one side, a missing hubcap on the other, and a large crack across the windshield. The glove compartment latch is broken so it's covered in strips of duct tape in order to make sure it stays closed (this feature is really the icing on the cake). Old Blue also has old-school doors. You know, the ones that don't open with the press of a button or the gentle pull of the handle (I would say handles, plural, but one of them broke off last week). The kind of doors that require a good, audible grunt to hoist them open, a simple fact that the ladies who run preschool drop-off/pick-up can't seem to remember as they stand on the curb waiting for a light to shine down from heaven and my doors to miraculously open on their own. Every. Single. Day. For four years. Amazingly, the doors still have to be opened manually. I say amazingly because the teachers look amazed/confused each and every time I roll down my passenger-side window (yes, my windows are electronic) and remind them kindly that they must, in fact, use their hands to physically open the van door. Once the door opens, I think the sweet teachers forget all about the lack of space-age technology (they become distracted by the minefield of food littering the carpet) because 99% of the time, they step back onto the curb after unloading my kids and wait for the doors to shut. Automatically. Which is literally impossible.

#SMH

I'm the mom who tells her kids to make their beds, but I can only seem to make mine on a good day or when my house is on the market.

I'm the mom who tells my kids to turn their underwear inside out and wear them again because (oops!) I forgot to move the laundry over to the dryer from the washing machine, resulting in stinky-drawers kiddos and a load of laundry that smells like death and must be washed again.

I'm the mom who forgets that the tooth fairy is supposed to come visit her first-born child for the very first time, so the next day, she grabs a wadded-up dollar bill from her wallet and carries it in to her daughter, explaining that the tooth fairy accidentally put her money in Mommy's purse and that it's warm and slightly damp because the tooth fairy has sweaty hands (ashamedly, I admit this is a true tale).

And sometimes...well, many times, I start to identify myself with my mistakes, taking them on as a part of me. Jordan, the mom who's always two steps behind. Jordan, the mom who embarrasses her kids. Jordan, the mom who forgets important things.

I'm sure you've never done this before, right? Wrong. We've all done it. It's so hard to escape the stranglehold our failures have on us, isn't it?

When we do this, we in essence rename ourselves, forgetting the name that has been given to us by our Heavenly Father. The only name that matters; the name that carries all of the weight and importance, that puts any name you and I can give ourselves to rest.

"Mine."

I believe He speaks the same words to us as mothers that He spoke to Israel through the prophet Isaiah so many years ago:

> *Fear not, for I have redeemed you;*
> *I have called you by your name; you are Mine.*

ISAIAH 43:1 (NKJV)

The Israelites of the Old Testament were riddled with failures and insecurities, and they deserved to be known for their mistakes. God, being the gracious, forgiving Father that He is, repeatedly took His prodigal nation back into His loving care, proving again and again that He is truly a God of redemption. The same God redeems us today, and it's in the moments we least deserve His love and acceptance that we find ourselves reminded of our name: "Mine."

When we allow our failures and weaknesses to define who we are, we start to engage in a very dangerous practice. What we tell ourselves becomes truth in our innermost beings, and lies can easily replace His truth and redefine who we believe ourselves to be.

If we're not careful, we can allow the lies of the enemy, the lies we allow to penetrate our hearts, to seep into the hearts and lives of our children. When we, as moms, aren't living in freedom and truth, how can we expect our children to do so? I am redeemed, even when I screw up my parenting and can't get my act together, and so are you.

Yes, I am that mom. No, I'm not a perfect mom. But I am their mom... ordained by my Heavenly Father to love and nurture and teach and, yes, sometimes even screw up the three tiny humans He chose to give to me. He could have given them to Mrs. Brady (forgive the '70s reference, but I honestly couldn't come up with a role-model mother in the current television era), but instead He gave them to me. And He gave your children to you.

We might drop off birthday gifts in flimsy plastic bags and forget a theme day at school. We may drive our kids around in a car that's a hot mess, and we may embarrass them in yoga pants and frizzy hair.

But.

They will always know that we're human. That we are broken. That we will never fully have our acts together. They must know our flaws and failures so they can see our desperate need for a perfect and faithful God, and for His grace that covers a multitude of sins, and maybe start to recognize the same need that dwells deep within themselves. Every time we screw up, our job is to point our kids back to the need for a holy, unblemished God whose forgiveness is enough for the vastness of our mistakes.

I have pointed my littles back to God more times than I can count, and I have generously supplied them with ample ammunition for the therapy they are sure to need as they enter adulthood.

#DontSayINeverGaveThemAnything

Who I'm Becoming (Hi, Mom!)

You know you're aging when you say something and you hear your mother's voice coming out of your own mouth. Talk about terrifying! This morning I literally said to my son, "I'll give you something to cry about, buster!"

I can now say with certainty that I'm turning into my mom. The first time I realized that I now embody my mother was a few summers ago when I totally narked on a bunch of teenagers who snuck into our neighborhood pool.

Let the implications of what I just wrote sink in for a minute. Let my utter uncoolness come into focus. Let the cringing begin.

Picture this, if you will: I'm relaxing with my family at the pool, just sitting down to eat a delivered-hot-at-the-pool pizza, when through the gate comes a posse of high schoolers ready to commandeer the pool. Yes, I said posse, but I'm not scared. I'm a grownup and they're weaklings. Really skinny, tan, bikini-clad weaklings, who I don't exactly dislike but also want to throw pizza at and hope they absorb the grease through their skin and grow muffin tops. Also there were some scrawny boys.

I immediately recognize one of the boys as the same boy who tried to sneak in a few weeks ago when he "forgot" his key. Our HOA board members told me about him and his friends, mentioned that their families had not paid their dues, and asked me to make sure that they don't use the pool. Trying not to be a complete loser I choose to ignore them and pretend like I don't see them.

In a matter of seconds, they have overtaken the pool and are doing twenty cannonballs per minute, turning our calm swimming hole into the Drake Passage. At this point, I'm only slightly irritated, hoping that by the time we finish our pizza, the novelty will have worn off and they will have calmed down a bit.

No such luck. As my kids finish eating and want to go swim again, I look over at the pool and see waves big enough to scare the crabbers on *Deadliest Catch*, and I instruct my kids to stay in the shallow end, far, far away from the giant, pubescent toddlers.

About this time, while I am putting my four-year-old's swim vest on, I hear one of the teenage kids yell, "JESUS!" And no, he wasn't having a revival. There are very few things in this world that truly bother or offend me, but that is one of them—and especially when my kids are listening. So you'll understand why my irritation turned to anger as my son yelled out, "JESUS," in true mynah-bird fashion. Nice.

I'm pretty perturbed at this point, not only over the swearing and the gigantic waves and the roughhousing, but also over the fact that my short-but-sweet family night is disintegrating before my eyes. So what do I do? Only what any patriotic, dues-paying Homeowners Association member would do if in my shoes: I call the president of the HOA and rat them out.

And in that moment, as though I was Cinderella and my fairy god-mother had cast a terrible, horrible spell on me, I turned into my mother.

Oh, there have been glimpses of my mother in me for years and years; however, it wasn't until this moment that it became unofficially official. There I stood, a thiry-something-year-old mom of three in a one-piece swim dress, calling the pool dictators and getting a bunch of teenagers in trouble for doing something I probably did at their age.

And I enjoyed it.

I don't mean that to sound cold or callous, but on some sick and twisted level, I liked narking on those kids. They were messing with my babies, so when my mama-bear instincts kicked in, I reacted. Right or wrong, I don't completely know, but one thing is for sure: I wanted to protect my children.

My mother would have done the same thing.

For years, I fought becoming my mother. Although she was, and is, amazing, I think that every young woman fights to be different, somehow desiring her own identity apart from the woman she calls Mother, no mat-ter how great or how awful her mother is.

My mother ~~couldn't~~ can't bake garlic bread without forgetting about it and burning it to a crisp, resulting in a smoke-filled kitchen and a wailing fire alarm that probably woke the neighbors and caused me massive hearing loss. I made it a goal to NEVER be so careless...I mean, how hard could it be?

My mother ~~was~~ is always covered in bruises. Not scary, DFACS-type bruises, but the kind one gets when missing a step and falling, or running into a light pole. She often talked about what an eyesore they were, so in my mind they were ugly and embarrassing and a physical reminder of clumsiness. I made it a goal to NEVER be so clumsy...I mean, how hard could it be? (Full disclosure: as I write this while sitting on the balcony of my stateroom, cruising quickly toward Mexico, it doesn't escape my attention that my left thigh is sporting a golf-ball size purple bruise that mysteriously appeared yesterday. The ironies never cease!)

My mother ~~killed~~ kills everything computer-related that she touches. She'll swear that she didn't "do anything," but somehow she has managed to wipe out more hard drives, lose more documents, and attract more viruses than I thought was humanly possible. I can't tell you the number of times I've called her, only to hear her answer my question of "what are you doing" with "I am waiting on a phone call back from a Mac genius to help me fix my _____." I made it a goal to NEVER be so technically challenged...I mean, how hard could it be?

Now I am in my thirties. I burn the garlic bread more often than I get it right. There is rarely a time when I am not sporting at least one or two deep-purple bruises on my arms or legs. I recently "synced" my iPhone with my laptop only to somehow lose all of my contact data, leaving me with a thousand random numbers and no names to put with them.

And then I narked on a bunch of teenagers who snuck into our neighborhood pool.

I could not be prouder.

You see, there is no one I'd rather be like than my mother. With every year that passes and every new stage of life I enter, I realize that becoming like Mom is something to strive for, not something to run from.

She is the godliest woman I have ever known. She is the wisest woman I have ever known. She is the loveliest woman I have ever known. And by the grace of God, may the same be said of me one day (although I am going to say that it might be a reach).

She epitomizes the woman described in Proverbs 31:10: Precious. Trustworthy. Hardworking. Providing. Strong. Tireless. Generous. Prepared. Crafty. Inventive. Dignified. Fearless. Wise. Kind. Caring. Excellent.

By her example, I have realized what it means to be a Christ-follower, a daughter of the King, and a mother to my three precious children. Now, more than anything, I desire to leave the same legacy of faith, love, and motherhood for my children, because I finally realize just how invaluable a gift that legacy is.

We all learn from our mothers, don't we? They're bound to impact us in profound ways, often positively, but also sometimes negatively. We model our parenting styles after their successes, and we do whatever it takes to avoid their failures. My mother wasn't perfect, a fact she readily claims, but she was honest and humble and teachable. And she loved us so deeply. When we as mothers devote our lives to our children and our children's children, the impact we'll have on future generations is incredibly far reaching and Kingdom-impacting, and it's a beautiful, beautiful thing.

By the way, my mom also loves to laugh. She can laugh at herself, and, as Proverbs 31 says, at the days to come. I think she's the one who gave me my sense of humor, and it's because of her that I can find humor in the ordinary things of life. I am thankful for a mother I can laugh with. And at. For instance, when accident-prone Mom cut her finger off for the second time in six months using the SAME vegetable mandolin, I laughed super hard. Wait, that doesn't sound funny, you say? Well, it was, I promise!

#GuessYouHadToBeThere
#SheWearsSteelGlovesNow

PHONE CALLS FROM PRESCHOOL

"Hi, Mrs. Watts. We're going to need you to come pick up your son, and you're probably going to want to take him straight to the doctor. You see, we were doing a craft project and instead of gluing the popcorn kernels we gave him onto his paper, he shoved them all into his ear canals. We tried, but we can't get them out. This has never happened before. So...yeah."

—Mrs. Z., preschool teacher and certified saint

II

Time

Phil: "Do you know what today is?"
Rita: "No, what?"
Phil: "Today is tomorrow. It happened."

—*Groundhog Day*

Quiet Time

Time is a funny thing. The older we get, the faster it runs out, or so it seems. Time is a commodity. It's more valuable than gold, in my opinion, and nothing highlights its importance quite like motherhood does.

The laws of time as I knew them changed forever on October 9, 2007. That's the day my daughter was born, the glorious, terrifying day when, miraculously, I lost over fifteen pounds in a matter of minutes. A lot of other great stuff happened too. But that quick weight loss is something else, huh?

I still remember how I felt in the hours and days that followed her birth. My insides were jumbled up as all of my lady parts shrank back down to size. I was 95% sure that I loved this little creature with the crazy eyes, and 78% sure that I actually wanted to take her home as my prize once my stay at the hospital's women's center was ~~yanked out from under me by my insurance carrier~~ finished.

One thing a woman can't grasp until she actually becomes a mother is how drastically her perception of time will change. Once I became a mom, I learned to sleep when I would normally be awake, to wake when I would normally be sleeping, to finish tasks in a fraction of the time it would have taken me when I was "just" a wife, and to do all of this while keeping my newborn daughter on a consistent schedule so that she would ultimately grow into a well-adjusted kid who sleeps at night.

I quickly realized that finding alone time, "me time," was going to be much more difficult than it had been in the past. Gone were the days of doing what I wanted, when I wanted. In order to have time for myself, I was going to have to make some serious sacrifices.

One area of my life that I have always tried extremely hard to prioritize is my time alone in the presence of God. I am nothing if not for His Spirit in me, and in order to walk daily in stride with Him I must, must, must spend time in His Word and in prayer. I am a morning person (by "morning person," I mean I peak between the hours of 9 a.m. and 11:59 a.m.). I have to have my time with the Lord in the morning because by 8:00 p.m., I am officially spent, both mentally and physically. Nothing ever gets accomplished after that except the folding of the occasional load of laundry. And the eating of ice cream.

Before I had children, my typical morning looked something like this:

7:30 a.m.: My alarm goes off and I hit the sleep button.

7:40 a.m.: My alarm goes off and I hit the sleep button.

7:50 a.m.: My alarm goes off and I stumble to the kitchen to get my cup of coffee, irritated and wondering why jobs have to start so dang early in the morning. (And let me just say, I was in MINISTRY. If you've been there, you know what that means: getting to work by 10:00 a.m. was usually quite acceptable, because you'd been spending time with the Lord before then.)

8:00 a.m.: With my Bible in hand, I'd settle in on the sofa with some nice worship music in the background, my hot coffee on the side table, and my journal and pen on my lap, ready to pray and listen to the voice of God. Overwhelming peace. Quiet. Tranquility.

Now, those of you with children read this and laugh. You laugh in camaraderie, followed up with a "oh-my-I-remember-those-days" sigh. You can probably still remember the mornings when the first sound you heard was birds chirping (because they had awakened before you) and the first sight you saw was bright rays of sunshine blazing through the cracks in your curtains. You remember the way you did things every day in their proper order: coffee, breakfast, teeth, shower, makeup, hair, clothes, go. These days, I'm lucky if I remember to brush my own teeth at all…because it takes ten minutes to brush my children's for them as they pitch a royal fit over whether they say "eeeeeeh" or "aaahhhhhhhh" while I do it. Tears are almost always involved.

After having children, everything changed about my quiet time. Everything.

I think that there is some kind of unspoken pact made among newborns while they congregate in the hospital's nursery. A pact to band together to make sure their parents know, beyond any shadow of a doubt, that they now rule the roost. That "bedtime" is questionable, that meals must be served promptly, and that when they say it's time to wake up, well, that is when it's time to wake up.

No one ever warned me of the laws of baby slumber. Something like, "She who wakes up will do so at the most inconvenient time." I always preferred Mark Twain's approach:

"Rise early, for it is the early bird that catches the worm." Don't be fooled by this absurd law; I once knew a man who tried it. He got up at sunrise and a horse bit him.[i]

After my daughter was a few months old and was sleeping twelve hours a night, and after I settled into a routine and recovered from the trauma that is becoming a first-time mother, I decided that I would start to…wait for it...wake up early for some time with the Lord. On purpose. Like, regularly. (I also said I was going to lose all of my baby weight before I got pregnant again, but that's another story.) I still remember my exuberance at the thought of being so disciplined that I was actually setting my alarm to get up before the sun. I just knew this was going to be a powerful time of communion with the Lord, since I was waking early and my daughter always slept until at least 7:00 a.m.

In my mind's eye, I saw my morning looking something like it had in days past...the coffee, the quiet, focused time with God. Instead, I am pretty sure it was more like this:

5:45 a.m.: My alarm goes off and I hit the sleep button.

5:55 a.m.: My alarm goes off and I stumble to the kitchen to get my cup of coffee, trying my very best to be as quiet as possible. As I enter the kitchen, I accidentally kick a chair, knocking it over and rattling the house. I fight the urge to drop a profanity and freeze, completely silent as I assess the damage. I hear no stirring from the baby's room, so I proceed with fixing my coffee.

6:00 a.m.: I tiptoe to my reading chair, turn on the dimmest light possible, wipe the dust off my Bible and journal, and sit down to be in the presence of God.

6:01 a.m.: I begin to pray.

6:02 a.m.: The baby cries. I ignore her.

6:05 a.m.: The baby cries harder. I start to feel rage.

6:10 a.m.: The baby is crying so hard that I'm starting to worry that she has a limb stuck between the slats of the crib, so I stop what I'm doing and go in to check on her. Upon my entry, she stops crying and grins. The end.

The next morning, I tried again. Only this time, I got up fifteen minutes earlier. So did the baby. Day three, same drill. I set my alarm even earlier. The baby did, too. Well played, baby. Well played.

And that was with only one child. Once Number Two came along, and then Number Three, the chances of everyone sleeping each morning until a reasonable time become slimmer and slimmer. Nowadays, I'm convinced that if I woke up at 2:30 a.m., the kids would be up and ready for breakfast by 2:45.

I remember when my youngest was still sleeping in a crib, and I woke up early to try and have some quiet time. The moment my rear end hit the chair, I heard my 23-month-old in his crib yelling, "No." Nothing else. Just "No." Over and over and over and over. Try listening to that for an hour while attempting to journal and pray. The fury that built up inside me threatened to overflow, and I wanted to punch something—anything. By the end of my "quiet time," I needed to confess my anger and beg for God's forgiveness, which is pretty funny considering that if I had just stayed asleep, I wouldn't have gotten angry to begin with and I would have looked way less tired that day.

There are times when I am beyond frustrated with this scientific phenomenon, times when I want to ask the Lord, "I mean, really? Don't You see, I'm waking up early, sacrificing my precious sleep, to spend time with You like You say I should? And You can't give them a dose of spiritual Benadryl to keep them in Sleepyland for even a few more minutes? What about MY quiet time?"

Then He gently whispers, "But my child, it's not about you."

You see, I don't think that having a "quiet time" makes us better Christians or more loved by God. He is not concerned with us checking off a list of the to-do items we've accomplished. He doesn't need our time. But He wants us to want Him. He wants us to want to spend time with Him. It brings Him joy to see us sacrifice what we would consider precious sleep to be with Him, even when there's not much that gets accomplished because of the chaos that is life with munchkins.

I think He wants to see that you and I trust Him.

I think it is less about how long our prayer times are and more about whether or not we really believe that He hears and answers the groanings of our hearts.

I think it is less about how eloquently our journals read and more about whether or not we are honest with Him in the few words we do write.

I think it's less about how many Scriptures we can cram in and more about chewing on the simple truths found in a small section of His Word.

I think it's more about the simply showing up. It's more about being available for Him, just saying, "I'm here."

Even as I write this, I must be honest and tell you that there are seasons when I quit. Sometimes, I don't even feel like trying. I grow discouraged, frustrated, and tired of not seeing the fruit of my sacrifice. So I place my time with Him on the back burner and opt for my solace to be found under a down comforter. And I get good sleep.

But in those seasons, I'm dry. I'm worn down. I'm tired, even though I am sleeping. And it's not worth it. It's just not.

Time will never again be what it was to us before we had children. What we once took for granted has become a precious and rare commodity, and we must make the most of it. And, most importantly, we must give our time back to the One who holds all time in His hands, the Alpha and Omega, the Beginning and the End. Because it's the least we can do when He gave it all for us.

One thing I ask from the Lord, this only do I seek:
that I may dwell in the house of the Lord all the days
of my life, to gaze on the beauty of the Lord
and to seek Him in His temple.

PSALM 27:4 (NIV)

I do have one quick tip for those morning quiet times. If your precious little one often awakens and decides to serenade you with a steady stream of crying as you pour your heart out to the Lord, I would urge you to visit your nearest drug store, where you can purchase a mega-pack of earplugs for under $3. These things really do the trick...you can tune just about anything out. They also come in handy on extended car trips.

Time Is Currency

People who know me, like, really know me, are well aware that I am a recovering extremist. Not in the terrorist sense, but more in the how-I-function-in-everyday-life sense. I am fairly certain I have OCD. Like, legitimately. Not the switching-the-light-on-and-off-fifty-seven-times-every-time-I-enter-a-room type OCD, but the kind where you are so obsessively focused on a task that you can't function in life until you complete said task.

Before I go any further, I should share that I come from a long line of people who are obsessive and/or compulsive. I'm fairly certain my own father starched and ironed everything he owned, even his underwear, for a long time (until the rest of my family and I made enough fun of him, like good family members do, that we shamed him into stopping). Growing up, my dad was known as "Habit Man." He's still, to this day, the only man I know who literally scrubs and sterilizes the kitchen sink before he starts to wash the dirty dishes. With a wet paper towel. That he then folds four times and drapes over the edge of the sink in case he should need it. Every. Single. Time. He. Does. The. Dishes. This results, to his credit, in a sink that shimmers like nothing you've ever seen.

It's not just my father's side of the family, though. My maternal side of the family is full of ~~anal~~ people who like things done a certain way each and every time. If you go to Ancestry.com and search under "OCD," I'm fairly certain that my entire lineage shows up. All of this is not to point fingers; it's simply to show that I come by my issues honestly. By that, I mean that it's honestly not my fault.

I love a clean house. I like an orderly life. I find it hard to think straight or accomplish anything if my home is in disarray, if there are chores to be done, or if there's half-finished work to be completed. I'm not the laid-back person who shrugs off all the mess and has all the fun because, NBD, it can wait until later. I find it hard to relax and let down when I know that things in my life or home or family or finances are not in order.

After having kids, my problems were exacerbated. A clean house is a sort-of non-option when you have small kids, which in and of itself can turn you into a looney toon. Cleanliness is automatically off the table. But even maintaining a neat house is enough to make a 33-year-old mom like me come unglued.

Not too long ago, we had the privilege of having new friends in our home. These friends had just moved to the USA from Egypt. They knew no one here; they had taken a leap of faith to immigrate to America to better their lives and the lives of their children. Having never been to the States before, this family packed everything they owned and moved to Atlanta, Georgia. They were lovely and kind. Their children were precious. They were strangers in a strange place who were eager to assimilate to our culture.

I spent much of the day preparing for our guests to come to dinner. I folded laundry. Like, ten loads worth (for reals). I dusted. I vacuumed. I straightened. I organized. And then, fifteen minutes after our friends arrived, I walked in to find my kids' room looking like a Hiroshima-sized toy bomb had been detonated.

In that moment, do you know what I wanted to do? (That I wanted to throttle my kids goes without saying, of course.) I wanted to sneak away to the kids' room and clean it up because it was eating away at my brain that their room looked like a hot mess after I had spent my time cleaning up the whole house earlier in the day. I wanted to leave my company with my darling husband (who hates to be left alone in social situations with strangers) and disappear into my boys' bedroom to make things neat and orderly again.

I honestly wanted to do that. Like, I had to fight the urge.

#ClearlyIHaveAProblem

And then something came to mind, something that my mother has said to me before and will probably need to say to me again a hundred times:

People matter before projects.

I had a living room full of people who needed to be welcomed and made comfortable and shown the love of a God they very probably didn't know. And all I could think about was the mess in the next room, a project that could be tackled at any time and that, in all honesty, didn't matter. I realized, thanks to the wisdom of my mother and the Holy Spirit allowing me to remember her words, that I needed to re-center my focus, and quickly. Immediately my stress over the Lego-and-matchbox-car explosion was diffused. Because, honestly, people matter before projects.

It makes me think about the time when Jesus visited Mary and Martha in their home. When Jesus arrived in town, Martha invited Jesus in to visit. It was, I'm sure, with grand intentions; I'm sure she wanted to serve Jesus and honor Him well. However, when Jesus came in and sat down, Scripture tells us that Mary spent her time sitting at Jesus' feet, listening to His teaching, while Martha was "distracted with much serving" (Luke 10:40). To top it off, Martha got upset that Mary wasn't helping her with the necessary chores, and she complained about as much to Jesus. When Jesus answered, His response was, to me, unforgettable:

Martha, Martha, you are anxious and troubled
about many things, but one thing is necessary.
Mary has chosen the good portion,
which will not be taken away from her.

Luke 10:41–42 (ESV)

In that moment, I think Jesus was trying to show Martha that stuff can wait. There will be time for stuff later. Stuff doesn't matter in the grand scheme of life. Jesus matters. Relationships matter. People matter. And people deserve our time.

I experienced a moment of shame that night as I saw the ugliness in my heart. Superficial, unimportant things fought for my attention—and almost won. However, I praise God that I am a work in progress and that He's not finished with me yet. I praise Him that the Holy Spirit whispered conviction to my heart before I wasted what turned out to be an invaluable time of pouring into people who desperately needed it.

In His goodness, He gave me the grace to release my unhealthy obsession with how neat and presentable my home was, instead giving me a love and a passion for the sweet people sitting across from me in my living room. He reminded me that people matter and that projects can wait, and that we are responsible to use our time for the Kingdom of God before serving our own ~~OCD~~ desires.

I'm kind of a selfish mess, and I'm guessing you are, too. Well, we can wait patiently for the day when we're perfected once and for all in the presence of our Savior, which is going to be fab, because I know that in that moment, we are not going to be thinking about our to-do lists. Instead, I'd like to imagine that I'll be frolicking, carefree, in some heavenly Alps-esque mountains like Julie Andrews did in the opening scene of *The Sound of Music*, worshiping the Lord of all creation with swirly, twirly dance moves that won't be remotely embarrassing because I'm in heaven. Also, I'm 99.9% sure that there won't be any messes in heaven because they are of the devil himself, which negates the need for cleaning.

That's #winning.

Doing Time

Whoever invented school breaks only did it for all the teachers out there.
#Truth

DISCLAIMER: If you're reading this during Spring Break while sipping a mojito on the beach in Sandestin as you watch your kids frolic in the ocean, you might just want to stop right here. Seriously.

All school breaks begin the same way in the Watts house. They are anticipated with the greatest of expectations. The Idealist Mommy in me starts by dreaming of sleeping in with no alarms set, and I plan fun breakfasts to make that take too much time to prepare on school days when everything is ~~coming unraveled~~ hurried. I plan play dates with friends and craft projects to do with the kids. I picture evenings spent watching movies and eating popcorn and staying up late while I cuddle with the kids on the sofa.

Those of you who know me can stop laughing now. The Idealist Mommy in me doesn't come out to play very often, and when she does, she's short-lived, mainly because reality sucker-punches me in the face. Let's take the art of breastfeeding, for example.

I was the mom who was sure I'd have breastfeeding in the bag. Since I'm not lacking in the breast department, I figured I'd naturally be a success. This was idealism at its finest. After my first child was born, it only took three weeks for reality to come and do a total number on me. It was a TKO, really. Two rounds of thrush for the baby AND for me (Google it, then gag), plus a round of double mastitis later, and it was formula for baby and antidepressants for me.

There was also the time I was sure it would be fun to take the kids bowling. Idealist Mommy whispered deep into the recesses of my mind that it would be a "Fun Family Saturday," and that once the glow of Cosmic Bowling fell upon my children, it would be an hour of utopian bliss. In reality, we arrived, spent twenty minutes trying to find shoes that fit my kids, and then walked toward the bowling lanes, passing the laser-tag arena on our way. My middle child decided then and there that he wasn't interested in the bowling we had yet to do and that all he wanted to do was play laser tag, so he spent the remainder of our time together crying on the bowling alley sofa. My youngest threw a fit because his shoes were ugly, and my daughter dropped her bowling ball on her foot.

Needless to say, an hour felt like eternity to my husband and me.

Last Spring Break, I had great plans, truly. My optimism lasted exactly two hours and seventeen minutes. And after the first day of Spring Break, my idealistic plans were out the window altogether.

Let's start with the plan to sleep in. Nothing wakes a mom up faster at 6:03 a.m. than the sound of glass magnets being thrown at the refrigerator by a four-year-old. I mean, who doesn't wake up at the butt-crack of dawn thinking it's a good idea to take all the magnets off the fridge and use them one by one to assault the faux-stainless patina?

The argument that followed between my two sons was a nice follow-up to the magnet episode. It was loud enough to wake my daughter, and I understand, really. Choosing whether to watch *Transformers* or *Inspector Gadget* is just cause for a heated debate at 6:05 a.m.

After I commandeered the remote control and chose a show that was neither *Transformers* nor *Inspector Gadget*, I went to work in the kitchen. I had a plan, a real treat for the kids. Homemade French toast, made with brioche and a yummy vanilla-bean sauce. It's not the kind of breakfast you make when you have ten minutes to get the kids out the door and off to school, so I was excited to take my time and try the new recipe. It smelled heavenly. It looked amazing. It tasted delicious. I dusted their plates with powdered sugar and drizzled warm syrup over the top of their toast, then called the kids to the table.

"Yuck!"

"What IS this?"

"I don't wike this for bweakfust," said the four-year-old, before even tasting a bite.

Oh, they'd like it. Yes, they would.

After they had gagged down their ~~disgusting~~ breakfast, I realized it was 7:17 a.m., and we still had the entire day in front of us.

#LordHelpMe

The rest of the day was full of activities. Activities like scrubbing toothpaste off the bathroom mirrors after Little Mr. Trouble decided to "paint" the glass from top to bottom. Like setting the kitchen timer in ten-minute increments as each of my kids inevitably rotated through the time-out circuit. Like trying to stay a step behind the kids to clean up their crumbs because our house was on the market and had to be ready for a showing at any time.

There was no crafting. No play dates. No family-movie-cuddle-time-lovefest to end the night. Heck, I put them to bed at 6:15 p.m. and set their clocks ahead two hours so they wouldn't argue with me about it.

#ThinkSmart

The thing is, this parenting gig is hard. And family time ain't always picturesque. I lose my patience and, as they so eloquently put it, "speak loudly" to my kids. They still hit and pinch each other. They call each other awful names like "Baby Chunkin" and "Doo-doo Head" and (my personal favorite) "Fart Face of Death." I make them do awful things like read books and clean up their rooms. I don't keep every craft my kids make, and I throw away most of their papers from school, which sometimes results in tears. But seriously, I don't want your page of addition and subtraction problems from yesterday, and the day before, and the day before that…

When you're a parent, the idea of a break is nothing but an illusion. Spring Break. Summer Break. Christmas Break. I personally think all school holidays should be renamed.

Spring Struggle. Christmas Confinement. Summer Servitude.

You may think I'm a bad mom for writing what you're secretly thinking. That's okay. You see, I know the truth. The truth is that I love my kids. I adore them. And I wouldn't trade the time with them for anything.

But that does NOT mean time together is ~~usually~~ always fun.

It's work. Hard work. And when everyone's home, together, all the time, it's harder and more work. A vacation, it is not. And that's okay.

My kids are worth the hard work, and so are yours. Scripture tells us that "children are a blessing from the Lord" (Psalm 127:3), that they are not mistakes, that God knitted each of them together in our wombs, and that they are "fearfully and wonderfully made" (Psalm 139:14). They are awesome, funny, sinful little creatures who are entrusted to us by our Heavenly Father to love to Jesus. I need these reminders from the Word sometimes when it seems like God missed a stitch or two.

Every time instructions are given to parents in Scripture, I've noticed that there's always a verb involved. A "do this" instruction. A call to action. Parenting is a constant state of doing, and doing is working. Therefore, parenting is hard work. And when everyone's home on "break," and there's loads of time spent together and no personal space happening, the workload is increased.

Bring it on. More time means more influence in my kids' lives. Even when I want to bail, I have to dig my feet in and love my kids to Jesus. And so do you. It's all that matters.

A refusal to correct is a refusal to love;
love your children by disciplining them.

PROVERBS 13:24 (MSG)

Young people are prone to foolishness and fads;
the cure comes through tough-minded discipline.

PROVERBS 22:15 (MSG)

Discipline your children; you'll be glad you did-
they'll turn out to be delightful to live with.

PROVERBS 29:17 (MSG)

Point your kids in the right direction-
when they're old they won't be lost.

PROVERBS 22:6 (MSG)

Take [your children] by the hand and lead them
in the way of the Master.

EPHESIANS 6:4B (MSG)

I know what you're thinking right now. Easy for her to say while she's sitting on the deck of a cruise ship sipping sangria and having loads of time to herself while she's "working" on writing this book. And you know what? You're right! It's SO much easier to say!

#DontBeAHater
#ItsOkYouCanHateALittle

STUFF MY KIDS SAY

"Mommy, smell my finger.
See, it smells nasty because I
stuck it in my bottom."

—*Sutton Watts, Age 4*

III

Patience

*"I sure was patient, Mom!
That was real good of me, wasn't it?"*

—*Emerson Watts, Age 5*

Pushing Buttons

My kids are good at a lot of things. One thing they are really, really good at is pushing my buttons. Trust me, I have several. The result of them exercising this particular talent is that I, in turn, want to press the nearest EJECT button and relocate myself to a sunny, secluded beach somewhere in a distant land, far, far away from those little button pushers.

It's truly amazing, isn't it? Kids seem to be born with the ability to push their parents' buttons, and to do so abundantly well. I sometimes think they don't even realize that they are driving us bonkers—that's how naturally button pushing comes to them!

One of my biggest pet peeves as a mother, if I can share this even while knowing it's so very trivial, is baby talk. Don't ask me why. I know there are bigger fish to fry when it comes to my children's heart issues and my parenting. That doesn't discount the fact that baby talk is just one of those things that makes me nutty.

My daughter used to be a world-class baby talker. She did it so well. And so often. It came in stages, but I knew we had reached an all-time baby-talking low when my daughter walked into the kitchen at age six and said, "Mommy, Emerson need to go pot-pot."

TRANSLATION: "Mom, I need to pee."

I winced immediately, hoping this was a one-time occurrence, just an accidental blip on the radar.

Wrong.

The days that followed were peppered with fun little goodies like:

"Mama, Emerson hungwy and want snacky-wacky."

"Mommy, me no want to go to bed. Me stay wakey with da mama."

"Wook, Emerson can eat her yogie with no hands," (as she sucked the yogurt off of her dinner plate like an anteater).

Pressing. My. Buttons.

I would hate for you to think that I have forgotten about my boys in this rundown, so I want to mention that they are also experts at pushing my buttons.

My middle child is a world-class loud talker. Even when there's no need, he finds it necessary to speak significantly louder than anyone else around. The worst is when we are in the van, enclosed and trapped. He loves listening to music and is always the first to ask me to turn on the radio. I do. He asks me to turn it up louder. I do. Just as I start to get into a song, singing along and relaxing now that all the kids are strapped into a moving vehicle and have nowhere to run:

"MOM!"

I turn the radio down calmly.

"Yes, son?"

"MOM, WHY DO THE RAINDROPS ON THE WINDSHIELD MOVE UP INSTEAD OF DOWN?"

I breathe slowly and resist the urge to rub my now-damaged ear.

"Well, son, it's because the air outside pushes against the raindrops when the car is moving and—"

"MOM! WHY IS THERE AIR OUTSIDE?"

Breathe.

"Well, son, because God knew that we needed air to breathe and so He—"

"MOM! TURN THE RADIO UP, PLEASE! I CAN'T HEAR THE MUSIC!"

Needless to say, my nerves are usually fried upon arrival at my destination.

If it were a competition, my youngest might have this in the bag. He's a child who likes four things to eat: peanut-butter-and-jelly sandwiches, fruit, goldfish (crackers), and candy. He eats those things (minus the candy) for lunch virtually every day. He eats them for breakfast most days, too. Then inevitably, when dinnertime rolls around and I bring a steaming hot plate of spaghetti and meatballs and chopped salad and garlic bread to the table, before a bite enters his cute little mouth, I hear, "I don't wike this food. It's yucky."

Blood. Boiling.

It could be anything. I have served him everything under the sun and he still doesn't "wike" it. Dinner often lasts hours for him at night while the rest of us go on with our lives; who knew it takes three hours for a four-year-old to eat two bites of chicken and a stalk of broccoli? He is not a big fan of our "try-three-bites-of-everything" rule, in case that wasn't clear.

How do they push my buttons with such precision?

Maybe the better question is: how can they not push my buttons?

They are children. It's their job to be ridiculously immature. And they do it like it's their job. They are supposed to talk like babies and act goofy. They are supposed to be loud. They are supposed to hate good food (that one might be a reach). Anyone who ever said children are to be seen and not heard obviously never HAD children, because that's just flat-out impossible.

They are children, and I get to be their mother. As their mother, I have a decision to make, a decision with weighty consequences. Am I going to allow my impatience, my petty peeves, to set the tone and the temperature for my lifelong relationship with my children? Am I going to major on the minors, picking at my kids? Am I going to allow my selfishness to make mountains out of molehills, exasperating my children in the process? Am I going to belittle them and strip away the CHILD out of their childhood by expecting them to function as tiny little adults?

Or am I going to let them be kids? Am I going to gently guide them, in love? Am I going to make them feel valued and important and wanted in spite of and no matter what they do? Am I going to show them how great I think they are JUST AS THEY ARE?

That's how God loves you and me, you know. As we are and not as we should be. I praise Him for that, because I will never be as I should be on this side of eternity. We have a Heavenly Father who takes patience to a whole new level, and He is the most consistent and loving parent there is. Maybe we should start by following His lead.

Lord, help me not to ever impose MY standards on my children, man-made standards that will teach them from an early age that they don't quite measure up to all that Mommy wants them to be. I feel like nothing will squash their joy and crush their spirits faster than this.

~~Fathers~~ Mothers, do not provoke your children to anger, but bring them up in the discipline and instruction of the Lord.

EPHESIANS 6:4 (ESV)

Notice that this verse does not say, "CHILDREN, do not provoke your PARENTS to anger." No, it's a directive to parents. God knows that kids will be kids. They will be immature. They will do stupid stuff. And they are somewhat off the hook for that because they are KIDS. We, though, as parents, are held accountable for how we respond to our children.

This verse says that we are to bring our children up in the discipline and instruction of the Lord. There are times to discipline our kids, most definitely. However, most of the button pushing in my house is frivolous, silly behavior, not sinful behavior. I am annoyed. And that is my problem, not theirs.

By the way, isn't it funny how surprised we act when our children hit us in our weak spots when we are guilty of doing the very same thing? I know there are times I pick at my husband, pressing his buttons just because I can, just because I know what riles him up. If I don't always have self-control as a grown woman, how in the WORLD can I expect my children to?

I want more than anything to keep my own expectations of my children in check and, instead, take on the expectations of the Lord as laid out in Scripture. I pray that as mothers, we can gain the patience we need to love our children through the annoyances and the awkwardness that comes with the job description, and that we can see them through the eyes of Jesus. I pray that as Christ followers, the Holy Spirit in us will give us wisdom to know when behaviors need to be addressed, when we're dealing with a heart issue, and when to just let it go. I pray that we learn to love our children through the challenging moments, following the example set for us by our Heavenly Father who so patiently and tirelessly loves us, His children.

So bring it on. Bring on the baby talk because there are worse things... my daughter could choose not to talk to me at all. Bring on the loud talking, because at least I can always hear my boy's heart clearly. Bring on the picky eating and complaining, because at least he feels safe enough in my home to voice his opinions. A lot of opinions. Often.

#BringItOn

Very Patient

If you are anything like me (and by now you're probably hoping you're not), you very well might utter the phrase "BE PATIENT" at least fifty-seven times per day. To your kids, to the dog, to your husband, maybe even to yourself.

"Son, if you interrupt me one more time while I am on the phone with the bank, I promise you things will not go well for you. BE PATIENT!"

"Sweetie, I know your brother wiped his finger across the dead frog and then stuck it in your face and told you to smell it, but that's no excuse to hit him in the face. BE PATIENT!"

"Self, I know you want to punch a hole in the sheetrock right now and that there is an intense rage inside you that is aching to be released, but BE PATIENT!"

Be patient.

Easier said than done, right? It's ~~funny~~ sad; I often become impatient while disciplining my own children because they were impatient. Yet another irony of motherhood.

All of that having been said, I have to brag on my daughter right now. She is not generally known for her patience. She asks for a snack and she expects it immediately, as evidenced by the repeating of the snack request every five seconds until said snack is prepared and provided. When I mention that I am taking her to see a movie later in the day, she asks every five minutes if it's "time yet." All. Day. Long.

About four years back, she had a great triumph over impatience. Unfortunately, it was in the wrong place and at the wrong time. Let me explain.

Picture this scene: it was about 9:30 in the evening and, in our home, this means that the kids had been asleep for about two hours. Brandon and I had been ~~doing our Bible study~~ watching *Survivor* (yes, that show is still on), and when it was over I suggested that we…uh…take a shower. Together. Hey, we are married, and married people have shower prayer time every night, right?

Anyway, we went in our bathroom, closed the door, and commenced to…showering. For a long time. Lots and lots of showering. (Wait, maybe I was wrong; do not picture this scene.)

After we "showered," we actually showered, and then we finally cut the water off. I opened my side of the curtain to lean out and get my towel and literally almost had a heart attack. Or slipped and fell in the shower. Or something.

Seated directly outside the shower, on her itty-bitty "Emerson" stool, was my four-year-old, with elbows on knees and chin in hands, staring. Just staring.

I screamed. Loudly. "EMERSON!"

I yanked the shower curtain closed and burst into nervous laughter. My husband looked shocked at first, and then, after seeing me nervously convulsing in naked laughter, he started laughing so hard that he couldn't breathe.

#NotHelping

I tried to compose myself (as if that was possible, as I was standing in the shower with her father after just having finished a long…prayer session), pulled the curtain back again, and poked my face out.

"Um…sweetie…uhhh…what are you doing in here? You're supposed to be in bed."

"Well, I woke up and I needed to talk to you, so I came to find you. I heard you and Daddy in the shower, and you said it's rude to interrupt adults when they're talking, so I just sat on my stool. Aren't you proud of me, Mommy? I was very, VERY patient."

Oh. My. Gosh.

At this point, my husband wasn't bothering to hide his laughter. I was on the brink of hysteria, thinking that I had certainly scarred my daughter for life.

"Well, how long do you think you were sitting out there, honey?"

She thought hard for a minute, then answered. "I don't know, Mommy. It felt like a long time. You guys were in there for forever, and you were talking VERY loud."

Yes, yes we were. Talking. Very loudly. Too loudly, obviously, when there are children in the house and our...talking...might wake them.

Then she asked me, "Mommy, why were you and Daddy getting a shower at the very same time?"

Well, dang.

"Because Mommy and Daddy were both very, very...dirty, Emerson. Yep, very dirty. That's why. Now go back in your room and get in bed, and I'll be there in a minute."

"Okay. But I sure was patient, Mom! That was real good of me, wasn't it?"

She hopped off of her stool and trotted back into her room.

I turned and stared at my husband. He was laughing so hard he was crying. I was terrified. I was sure that the next time her preschool teachers asked her to fill in one of those "My Parents..." surveys, hers was going to say something like, "My mommy's favorite thing to do is...to get in the shower with Daddy when they are very, very dirty."

She, of course, hasn't mentioned the incident ever again. She must have forgotten. Either that or the story is now stored in her arsenal for use at the perfect time in the future. And we, of course, now double-check the locks before...praying together.

In all seriousness, though (if that's even a possibility now), my husband and I try to focus on creating a patient atmosphere in our home. We encourage our children to be long-suffering. We try to teach them that what is immediate is not always what is best, that sometimes we have to be patient in order to really get what we want. We used to have a long hallway, and in that hallway I painted a tree. Let me say right off the bat that it was fairly unattractive, hence the reason that I refer to it in the past tense (we have since painted over it and moved to another home). I am not a painter. However, we wanted a fruit-of-the-spirit tree in our hallway, so paint I did. Patience is one of the fruits of the Spirit, and my husband and I used its presence on the tree to reinforce its importance every chance we got with our children. The problem was that, when referring to my artwork while trying to teach the children, they often got stuck on the fact that "patience" was a bunch of grapes, and that grapes don't grow on trees. Yeah, well, neither do watermelons, but we had one of those on our tree, too. Mama's not a painter or a farmer, so lay off.

The problem is that, with three small kiddos, patience is often hard to come by. It's easily taught but not easily retained. They struggle with it. I struggle with it. It's a daily battle.

God's Word encourages us all, young and old, to practice patience in all that we do. God sets the example for us:

The Lord is slow to anger and abounding in steadfast love,
forgiving iniquity and transgression…

NUMBERS 14:18 (ESV)

But You, O Lord, are a God of compassion and mercy, slow
to get angry and filled with unfailing love and faithfulness.

PSALM 86:15 (NLT)

He is so good, and He is 100% consistent in His patience with us. Then it's our turn to learn from Him and to exhibit His qualities as a child does his father's. The Bible tells us in Colossians 3:12–13 (ESV):

Put on then, as God's chosen ones, holy and beloved,
compassionate hearts, kindness, humility, meekness, and
PATIENCE, bearing with one another and, if one has a
complaint against another, forgiving each other; as the
Lord has forgiven you, so you also must forgive.

It's a tall order. It's a lot of work. It's not, by any stretch of the imagination, easy. But imagine how our children might grasp the power of patience if they were to watch you and me treat others with the very same attitude, extending them grace and loving them with holy love. It's a challenge, but it's one that I believe we can and should accept. So who's with me? If you desire to see patience and peace reign in your home, I'd encourage you to pray right now that the Lord will begin the necessary heart change in you and your husband. Go ahead, feel free to pray.

One more thing: I would recommend very highly that all doors be locked and all fart-fans turned on to drown out the "talking" next time you and your husband decide to "pray" together in the shower. You're welcome.

<u>STUFF MY KIDS SAY</u>

"Mommy, today in Sunday school my teacher said Jesus went on a boat and He was real tired and He went to sleep and it was raining real hard and the guy was scared. Then Jesus woke up and He turned into a pirate."

—*Emerson Watts, age 4*

IV

Chick-Fil-A

*"We didn't invent the chicken,
just the chicken sandwich!"*

—*Chick-fil-A*

I am, proudly, from the birthplace of the original chicken sandwich—or at least the best chicken sandwich. Atlanta, Georgia: home of Kris Kross (may he rest in peace), Lil Wayne, Julia Roberts, Home Depot, Coca-Cola, and all of the goodness that is Chick-fil-A. There are very few things that excite my taste buds as much as a spicy chicken sandwich with a freshly carbonated straight-from-the-fountain half-Coke-half-Diet-Coke split. If you're not from the South and you wonder to what culinary masterpiece I am referring, well: #1) I pity you, and #2) I say head south. There's nothing like a southern-fried chicken sandwich, and it's worth the drive!

My family frequents Flick-fil-A, as we affectionately call it, on a regular basis. Their restaurants have fabulous indoor play areas for kids where we have spent many a rainy morning. One experience, however, stands out from the rest. One fateful evening is forever etched in the deep recesses of my mind. One experience left me so emotionally scarred that I felt border-line homebound for days, fearful of reentry into society. This is the story of the (first) time my children terrorized Chick-fil-A.

It was a Saturday evening sometime in September of 2011. My dear, sweet husband was attending a conference for the weekend, which meant that I was single-mothering it with a three-year-old, a two-year-old, and a three-month-old. Unless you're a single mother (and don't worry, you'll get a shout-out a bit later in the book), moms out there know how it feels to get to Friday, that glorious, heaven-sent Friday, when the weekend is upon you. Daddy will be home to tag-team baby duty, and Mom can get some semblance of rest and recuperation.

Moms also know how it feels to have a disruption in the routine, a weekend when Daddy is away. I am not diminishing the importance of our hubbies getting away every now and then, but neither am I diminishing the stress it puts on us as moms to move from one week into the next without any sort of a break from the normal grind. (Again, hats off to you, single moms. You're rock stars for soldiering through, week after week, without a break. And you inspire me.)

This particular weekend had been rather crazy at our house. Brandon left for his conference early on Saturday morning, while I ran around like a crazy lady, dressing and feeding the kids and packing up to drop them off at my mother's house so that I could go throw a baby shower. It's always fun to start a Saturday morning in hose and heels, right? I even had a minor squabble with my husband as I had to call him one minute after his class started to ask if he had my car keys—apparently a very inconvenient interruption that was super-annoying to him. But I couldn't leave home without the keys. To throw a baby shower. That I was in charge of. Yet he was the irritated one.

#Sigh

At any rate, after a crazy, non-stop day, dinnertime snuck up on me, and I found myself without an ounce of energy to prepare a meal for my kids. No problem, because there's always Chick-fil-A! How can one go wrong with chicken nuggets and "lemolade," as my middle son affectionately used to refer to it?

I load my kids into the van, and off we head to devour some fried-chicken goodness. We arrive at Chick-fil-A, and I begin the process of unloading all three children, including the baby in his infant carrier. I get all three children into the restaurant and order dinner, get them all situated, and settle in for an easy, yummy dinner (insert foreboding, evil laughter here).

After one chicken nugget, both of my older children announce that they are no longer hungry, that they want to get down and go play (there are blessings and curses to eating in a restaurant with a playground, am I right?). The same children who were "starving" just moments before, weeping and wailing over the three-minute wait for dinner, declare themselves full. This is a universal parenting phenomenon, is it not? At any rate, I allow them to go play because, if for no other reason, I can finally have a few moments of peace. And honestly, what do I care if they eat cold nuggets later?

While I watch my older children play in the glassed-in cage playground, I decide to go ahead and feed my newborn his bottle. For a few moments, the world is at peace. The kids are playing, the baby is eating, and I zone out, probably with a small stream of drool dripping from my mouth as exhaustion sets in.

Then I feel it. Warmth. And I smell it. An unmistakable smell. Baby poop

The baby appears to be enjoying his bottle so much that he fills his diaper to make room for more milk in his precious little belly. Fill it he does. His proverbial cup runneth over.

I lift him up to find that he is covered in runny, nasty baby poop—and so is the front of the dress that I am still wearing from the baby shower I hosted earlier in the day. My heart sinks, but I refuse to panic. I look around for the diaper bag, quickly realizing that I left it in the car. Of course I did.

I debate grabbing the kids out of the play area, but that would just add to the chaos...so I ask a random woman sitting next to me if she would mind making sure my children didn't escape the play area while I run out to the car to get the diaper bag. She obliges, so I grab the baby and run out to the car to get clean-up supplies for this poop situation.

I run back into the restaurant and brazenly ask the unassuming woman if she would mind helping me once more; will she please keep an eye on the two playing children while I run to the bathroom to clean up the baby and myself? She agrees, this time a little more warily, but I hear a "yes," and I take it.

In the restroom, I strip the baby down to nothing, wash him off, and diaper him. He has no other clothes, so we have no choice but to go red-neck-style (diaper only). I try rinsing the green poop out of my dress but, having little success, I give up and head out of the restroom to get the big kids and hurry home.

It is about this time, as I am exiting the restroom and heading back to my table, that the poor, random woman charged with watching my big kids comes walking toward me with my three-year-old daughter in tow.

Random Lady: "Um, Ma'am, she says she had an accident."

Me: "What kind of accident?"

Random Lady: "She says she wet her pants."

With one look, it becomes painfully apparent that my daughter is telling the truth; I see that her shorts are soaked through and still dripping.
This. Is. Not. Happening.
"Sweetie," I ask her, "what happened? When did you tinkle in your pants?"
She answers back in a matter-of-fact tone, "I couldn't hold it, so I tinkled up at the tippity-top of the playground."
Yes, that would be the same playground that is currently overrun with at least a dozen children.
This is about the time when the angel and demon both come out to play. The demon on one shoulder tells me to grab my kids and get the heck out of Dodge, to leave before anyone can realize what has happened. The angel tells me that, no, I must do the right thing and report this to the authorities. Darned angel.

I tentatively walk up to the counter where two teenage girls are ~~talking~~ working, and I say as quickly as I can, "I'm so sorry, but my daughter just peed in the playground."

Both girls stop talking and stare at me for a moment. I'm sure they are processing what I just said. The looks on their faces are priceless, and I wish I could take a snapshot to enjoy later. Girl A then turns to Girl B and says, "Well, I'm sure as h#@l not cleaning it up!"

The other girl looks embarrassed by her coworker's behavior and reassuringly tells me not to worry, that they will take care of it. I apologize profusely and then go to grab my remaining child, my then-two-year-old son, from the playground so we can leave.

On our way to the play area, I stop at our table to put the clothing-optional baby back in his carrier and leave him there. He hates his carrier. He screams and wails. Whatever.

I enter the playground and call to my son, "Sutton, it's time to come down and go home!"

As I am hollering, in behind me walks two employees. One has a sign she tapes to the door that reads:

PLAYGROUND CLOSED DUE TO CONTAMINATION.

The other employee shouts out the door to all parents in the vicinity, "Parents, please clear your children out of the play place; we must close it due to a child having desecrated the area with her urine."

Okay, she doesn't say that exactly, but she does tell them to get their kids out, that the playground is closed for the night because "some" kid peed up at the "tippity-top."

Parents rush in to get their children. A little girl comes down the slide to her mother, causing her mother to scream in horror, "Oh, honey, you're covered in URINE!"

I feel like telling her to calm down, that at least urine is sterile, as proven by Bear Grylls when he ended the debate once and for all. However, I think that offering unsolicited advice like this might earn me some slashed tires, so I use self-control.

I continue to call my own son down from the very top level of the maze, to no avail. After a moment or two, I realize that I am the only parent left in the play area, the only parent with a child that refuses to obey and come down. He has decided in this moment to wage war against his mother. He. Is. Not. Budging.

I start threatening the pain that is soon to be inflicted on his rear end if he doesn't choose obedience, a threat at which he laughs. Again, I call him down. Again, he says no.

My daughter is now crying at my side because her shorts are wet and she is cold. The baby is still crying in his infant carrier on the other side of the glass. People are staring. And a two-year-old is holding me hostage.

At this point, I do what any other fed-up mother would do in a dire situation. I kick off my heels, and I start to climb. Up the spiral staircase. Through the tunnel. Up the net. To the very "tippity-top" where my son is cowering in the corner, quickly realizing the fate that is awaiting him. I grab him and hurl us both down the twirly slide, which shoots us out onto the ground below. I grab our shoes and march all three of us out of the play area to get the neglected baby, who at this point is out-of-control crying while a "new" random lady rocks his infant seat in hopes of calming him down. I realize that we have gained quite an audience watching us on the other side of the glass.

Feeling the burn of people's glares, I breathe that evil-whisper, I-sound-possessed type thing we moms do, and tell my children to get their dag-gum shoes on and stop fussing. As I bend down to help my son velcro his shoes, my daughter stands and picks up her chocolate milk from the table. She turns around and instantly drops it. As the almost-full bottle of chocolate milk hits the ground, it explodes onto every single table and person in the general vicinity. There are very few ways you can drop a bottle of milk to make it explode up and out like that. She does it right.

#IWishIWereMakingThisUp

In the words of *The Office*'s lovable Jim Halpert, Lord, beer me strength.

With all three children in tears and baby carrier in hand, I march back up to the counter, this time totally beyond caring what the employees think, to let them know that we have a "slight" problem near our table, a milk explosion of sorts. The girls just stare at me. I stare back.

My two-year-old decides to tell me at that moment that he wants ice cream. This is coming from the kid who made me scale, in my church dress, what felt like Mt. Everest. This is a gutsy request, if you ask me. And since he did ask me, I answer him. "No." And not only no.

He apparently doesn't like my answer much. He lies down on the floor in the middle of the line of customers waiting to order their delicious chicken dinners and proceeds to pitch the world's loudest and ugliest temper tantrum. He is so out of control that I am physically unable to calm him, seeing as how I'm holding an infant carrier in one hand and dragging my blubbering pee-soaked three-year-old with the other.

That's when I start to cry, too. If you can't beat 'em, join 'em, right?

At this moment, the Lord intervenes and an angel, disguised as a Chick-fil-A manager, has compassion for me. He comes around the counter and scoops up my son, offering to carry him to the car for me. I smile at him through my tears and, together, we somehow get everyone safely to the car, where we physically restrain them.

I climb into the driver's seat with poop still smeared all over the front of me, a cold, crying daughter behind me, and a two-year-old next to her, still begging for ice cream. The baby has conked out at this point, probably too traumatized to stay awake any longer.

It takes everything in me not to curl up in the fetal position and start the shut-down sequence. I pull out of the parking lot and begin the drive back home, listening to the repeating chorus of "I'm hungry" and "I'm cold" the entire trip.

I pull into the driveway to find my husband's car parked there. He is home. Oh, boy, is he going to be sorry that he is home. I march the kids to the front door, ring the doorbell and, as he answers, I shove our precious angels at him, announcing that he is "on." I dare him to contradict me as I stare him down. He sees the pure fury in my eyes and doesn't say a word;

he simply takes the children, ushers them to the bathtub, knowing well enough to steer them clear of me for the remainder of the ~~century~~ night.

Later that night, after I have a few ~~glasses of wine~~ hours to cool down, he sits down across from me.

"What happened?" he asks.

"You don't want to know," I reply.

"Yes, I really do," says my superhero husband.

After unloading the ugly details on him (while he tries to hold in his laughter), I sigh and say, "I just wish we had normal children. Not the kind of children that act out. Not the kind of children that speak their minds. Not stubborn-as-mules kids. No, the kind of children that are seen and not heard, the kind that are EASY."

In that very moment, I hear the Holy Spirit speak to the innermost parts of me.

"No, you don't."

And He is right.

You see, if I am honest with myself, I don't want robotic children who make parenting super-easy while at the same time suck the joy out of the very life we are trying to build. I don't want quiet, subservient children that are seen and not heard, that are afraid to be themselves and to stand apart from the crowd. I don't want to raise human beings with no fight in them, people who aren't willing to dig in their heels for something they really believe in and duke it out to the end. I want them to be stubborn for the sake of the gospel, for the sake of truth, and for the sake of what and Who they believe in.

I could have done without the stubbornness at the "tippity-top" of the slide from my son, but hey, you win some and you lose some, right?

Honestly, even though the experience we had at Chick-fil-A that long-ago evening was horrific (and it really was), when I look back, I wouldn't trade that amazing, no-one-will-believe-this string of events for anything in this world, because through it, the Lord allowed me to realize that I am no different from my kids.

No. Different.

I mess up, and when the you-know-what hits the fan, the first person it usually hits is my Savior. I am really good at allowing my sin, my nastiness, to taint people's perception of who He is. I mess up, it's obvious. And unfortunately, I can make Him look pretty bad.

I am also stubborn. He calls me down from a place where I am not supposed to be and, instead of listening and obeying, I dig in my heels and refuse to come down. He is good enough to climb to my rescue, not leaving me there to fend for myself; but in my disobedience, I end up having to reap consequences that He never desired me to have.

I throw temper tantrums when I don't get ice cream. Okay, maybe not ice cream, but I have been known to pitch a fit when my comforts are not catered to. When I am inconvenienced. When the answer He gives to a prayer is not the answer I wanted. I am as spoiled as my son appeared to be that night at Chick-fil-A.

And yet He made me—and you—this way. He made us with wills and with dreams and with tempers and with stubborn streaks when He could have made us robotic, unfeeling worshipers. Why did He do this?

Because there's just about nothing worse than a manufactured relationship with the ones you love. What good is it to love another if you don't see them for who they really are, even if it means you're forced to see the worst in them?

I believe this is how the Lord feels about us. He wants us to be free to be ourselves as we learn and grow in our walks with Him, and as we learn more and more what it looks like to live and love like Jesus. It's because of the gift of the cross that we have this freedom. No more rules. No more rigidity.

This is the same thing I want for my children. No façade of perfection is going to give us depth in our relationships with one another. Just because it's easy doesn't mean it's worth it. And because I love my children, I need moments like the one at Chick-fil-A.

One of my favorite sections of Scripture, found in Galatians 2:17–21 (MSG), supports this argument:

Have some of you noticed that we are not yet perfect?
(No great surprise, right?) And are you ready to make
the accusation that since people like me, who go through
Christ in order to get things right with God, aren't perfectly
virtuous, Christ must therefore be an accessory to sin? The
accusation is frivolous. If I was "trying to be good,"
I would be rebuilding the same old barn that I tore down.
I would be acting as a charlatan.

What actually took place is this: I tried keeping rules and
working my head off to please God, and it didn't work. So
I quit being a "law man" so that I could be God's man.
Christ's life showed me how, and enabled me to do it.
I identified myself completely with him. Indeed, I have been
crucified with Christ. My ego is no longer central. It is no
longer important that I appear righteous before you or have
your good opinion, and I am no longer driven to impress
God. Christ lives in me. The life you see me living is not
"mine," but it is lived by faith in the Son of God, who loved
me and gave himself for me.
I am not going to go back on that.

Is it not clear to you that to go back to that old rule-
keeping, peer-pleasing religion would be an abandonment of
everything personal and free in my relationship with God?
I refuse to do that, to repudiate God's grace. If a living
relationship with God could come by rule-keeping, then
Christ died unnecessarily.

Lord, may we be identified completely with You, with egos that are crushed under the weight of Your gift of grace. May we learn to live in relationship with You, real relationship, and not hide under the façade of perfection. And may the same be so for our children.

PHONE CALLS FROM PRESCHOOL

*"Hi, Mrs. Watts. I'm sorry to have to call and tell you this,
but Foster bit Connor a few minutes ago because he wanted
the green Matchbox car. Thankfully, it didn't break the skin.
Normally we'd send Foster home, but since he wants to come
home so bad, I'm just going to make him stay here."*

—*Mrs. Z., preschool teacher and certified saint*

V

Real

"'[Real] doesn't happen all at once,' said the Skin Horse. 'You become. It takes a long time. That's why it doesn't happen often to people who break easily, or have sharp edges, or who have to be carefully kept. Generally, by the time you are Real, most of your hair has been loved off, and your eyes drop out and you get loose in the joints and very shabby. But these things don't matter at all, because once you are Real you can't be ugly, except to people who don't understand.'"

—MARGERY WILLIAMS, *The Velveteen Rabbit*

Grace and Scarlett

If I'm honest with you (and remember, I promised you that I would be, for better or worse), thus far my life has been comprised of many a series of unfortunate events. This is not to say my life has been completely unfortunate; it's quite the opposite, actually. I have really enjoyed navigating my way through my 30- *(cough)* something years. I just happen to trip and fall from one phase of life to the other, usually without finesse, and usually in front of lots of people. I always get where God wants me to go, but I'm not exactly elegant or discreet about it; if I were, I'd have no material from which to pull while writing this epic piece of literature. And where would the fun be in that?

Some people seem to float through life so skillfully, don't they? Quiet and demure, always saying and doing the right things. Always socially acceptable and well-mannered. Never tripping over guitar cases and landing on their stomachs onstage in front of a few thousand people. Wait, has that not happened to you? Anybody? It's just me?

Life's a breeze for those people, or so it seems to those of us who belong to a clumsy band of misfits who stumble through life somewhat awkwardly.

For the sake of illustration, let's refer to the floaters as "Grace." As in Grace Kelly. You remember Grace, don't you? Ladylike. Polished. Charming. She wasn't named Grace for nothing. I'll bet you a million dollars she never tripped over a guitar case and fell on her stomach onstage in front of a few thousand people.

#ObviouslyIHaveSomeIssuesToDealWith

Then there's me, and maybe you, too. We're the misfits. The foot-in-the-mouth, loud-talking, accident-prone, somewhat-awkward misfits. The ones I affectionately refer to as "Scarlett."

Why Scarlett, you ask? Well, I've referred to my clumsy, awkward side as Scarlett ever since the time Scarlett Johansson (the actress) tripped and fell in front of the paparazzi in New York City in literally the strangest position possible. And they captured it on film. And now it's a national treasure. (Go Google it right now, for real.) We misfits remember this moment vividly, probably because we were just relieved that we weren't the ones who had fallen (that time, anyway). You remember this, I'm sure. If you don't, then you're probably named Grace, and you probably only watch cable news channels and spend your time dwelling on intelligent things.

Scarlett got more publicity for her "have a nice trip, see ya next fall" debacle than she has for any movie role in recent memory. She was all over the internet. Soon, there were more photoshopped pictures of her than of the Grumpy Cat (again, Grace, for your benefit I will translate: that's a lot of photoshopped pictures). The images were priceless: Scarlett sliding into first base: SAFE! Scarlett riding a killer whale. Scarlett crawling out of the crumbled earth along with several other mutilated zombies from *The Walking Dead*.

Pictures like these remind me of the times when this Scarlett (that's me) crashed and burned. Like that time when the tread peeled off of my super-fly platform heels on Easter Sunday and I didn't know it and I walked down the main aisle of my 5000-member church only to slip and fall, again on my stomach, this time in an Easter dress? Or maybe like the time I was seven months pregnant and I fell down the basement stairs and had to be hospitalized for my clumsiness? What about the time I was taking a Boot Camp exercise class with about thirty other women and our instructor sent us to the track to run laps and I tripped over...well, nothing, and I did a double somersault before smacking my face into the wall? I mustn't forget to mention the time I threw a ball in our front yard for our chocolate Labrador to fetch while I was still holding his leash (I still don't know what the heck I was thinking) and he took off after it like a dog chasing a ball does and I, in turn, was pulled straight into the metal pole that held up our carport, resulting in a split-open eyebrow and a knot on my face the size of a softball. I looked especially pretty on the large HD screens at church the following morning as, of course, I was booked to lead worship less than twelve hours after said accident. Or like...well, you get the idea.

Oh, Scarlett.

What about the time when I was fighting a deep depression and I couldn't claw my way out and I was stumbling around the darkness, falling again and again and again? And I stumbled in my walk of faith, and I didn't know if I believed. And I entertained doubts about the One Person who has always proven consistent and true in my life.

God refined me through that season, and I walked into a more mature relationship with Him after the battle, but I'm not without scars. I stumbled my way from childlike faith into a deeper walk, but it was messy. It took a pursuant God and Prozac. I wasn't Grace.

What about the time when I was so insecure about my physical self that I indulged an eating disorder and a mind disorder to "fix" myself? When I stumbled into an exercise addiction that had a grip on me like nothing ever has, when I chose superficial beauty and unattainable perfection over an internal, eternal radiance. I wanted to be Grace, but instead I was going down like Scarlett, and I couldn't see what was happening right in front of my eyes.

God reached down and pulled me out of what could have been incredibly damaging to me, emotionally and physically, but I am not without my fair share of wounds. I tried to make myself acceptable instead of allowing Him (and others) to love me as I was.

What about the moments, even now, when my selfishness overtakes my servanthood and I sin against my children and my husband because I care more about me than them? I stew in anger and relive the injustices of being used and disrespected over and over again, all the while building my case for why I "deserve" a break, deserve better. Then I see myself for the horribly selfish sinner that I am and I repent and vow to give myself away just as Christ did for His church. And then one of my children disrespects me and I begin to simmer again.

Grace would make homemade cookies every day and never respond in anger and always respond with a sing-song voice to her little rascals. But I am not Grace; I'm Scarlett. I fall and I fail, time and time again.

Here's the thing I keep coming back around to: if I were Grace, I don't know that I'd need my God like I do when I'm Scarlett. Grace doesn't need to be picked up and dusted off to try again; she simply doesn't fall in the first place.

I am Scarlett. I stumble and fall. I grow weary. I'm sad. I'm selfish.

I'm a sinner, and I'm in need of a Savior.

With Him, I can walk freely as Scarlett, knowing that even when I crash and burn, my God will be right beside me, gently picking me up, dusting me off, and setting my clumsy feet back on the road toward heaven. I will not be Grace this side of heaven, but if I need God and I know God, then I am saved.

The steps of a man are established by the Lord, when he delights in His way; though he fall, he shall not be cast headlong, for the Lord upholds his hand.

PSALM 37:23–24 (ESV)

Truth be told, I'd rather be Scarlett, stumbles and all. At least we Scarletts know how much we need a perfect Father. And I rest in knowing that I will be Grace, the epitome of beauty and perfection, when I set foot in eternity (and not a moment before).

P.S. Grace doesn't really exist in this fallen bunch of misfits we call mankind. Just FYI.

P.P.S. Scarlett Johansson was not harmed in the writing of this chapter. Seriously, she doesn't even know who I am. And she's mega-rich and she probably sopped up her tears with her wads of cash when she fell that day in NYC.

Spiritual Spanx

I spend a lot of time thinking up ~~brilliant~~ things. I have thought to myself more than once, "Self, you should really be a millionaire by now with all of your fantastic dreams and visions and ideas and inventions. You should maybe even go on that show *Shark Tank* to get some investors. Yeah, then you'd really be able to make things happen!"

Then I realize (thanks, mainly, to Google searches) that I will not be a millionaire from said ideas. Because someone else already is. I missed having a corner on the market by *this* much.

One time, as my cousin and I sat around talking, we came up with a brilliant product. We were going to call it "The Fridge Friend," and we were sure it was going to be a hit. It was, to keep things basic, a pad of paper with a magnet on the back that you hang on your refrigerator to mark down all sorts of things like grocery lists, to-do tasks, phone calls that need to be made, etc. Yes, I know there are products like this already in existence that are produced by large companies such as Real Simple and MomAgenda and every planner-printing company ever. Yes, I know (in retrospect) that it was a horrible idea, mainly because products just like The Fridge Friend could be found at every big-box store and specialty paper shop. But we were sure ours was going to be the product every woman wanted. Because it was

The Fridge Friend. We even bought a domain name. I have nothing else to say about that.

I swear I invented the ShamWow. Long ago, I thought to myself, *Self, wouldn't it be fabulous if there was a cloth SO absorbent that it could clean up virtually any mess and leave behind no residue?* Then, lo and behold, during my HGTV marathon one evening many years back, the ShamWow graced my television screen, leaving me speechless (and some other dude mega-rich).

I am also pretty sure I invented the spork when I was four. I remember wanting to tape my spoon and my fork together to make something my mother had cooked easier to eat. Genius! Not long after that, my family visited a local Kentucky Fried Chicken, and what did they include with our meal but a spork. [For the record, I would have totally called it a foon; it's shorter and more to the point(s).]

#SeeWhatIDidThere

Disclaimer: Items I did not invent (but someone else did), for the sake of my reputation, are the following (you can Google them—they're for real):

- Handerpants (underpants for your hands; otherwise known as fingerless gloves)
- Diet Water (because it's a real drag when regular water makes you fat)
- Aqua Notes (a notepad that hangs on the shower wall so you can multitask while shampooing, because, let's be honest, there's no need to maintain reverence for the single last place on earth where one can be alone and at peace for five minutes a day)
- The Candwich (yes, it's just what it sounds like—a sandwich in a can)
- The Kitty Wig (for those times when you want to dress your cat up in a long, pink wig and simultaneously achieve maximum weirdness as a human being and animal owner)
- The Shake Weight (just...why?)

I think that before I ever invented anything, I would have to ask myself, "Self, is this product something that could ever be the subject of a parody on *Saturday Night Live*?" If the answer is yes, the idea will be 100% disregarded. If the answer is no, then it has probably already been invented, making someone else filthy rich.

I must make a confession. If I could have invented anything in the world, anything at all (besides cures for AIDS and cancer and free ways to purify water globally and a robot to do all of my housecleaning), I would have created Spanx. You know what I'm talking about. You probably have a pair of them in your undergarment drawer, right next to your Handerpants. Spanx are, simply put, the greatest of all inventions, ever. (Side note: if you're super thin and don't have an ounce of fat to compress, you need to go on ahead and skip to the next chapter, because Spanx don't work for bulging pelvic bones or protruding ribs; they're for "fluffy" girls like me. So…bye, Felicia.)

With Spanx, clothing fits differently. Awkward lumps are replaced with perfect and soft feminine curves. A woman feels confident and empowered when she wears Spanx because she knows that no one is going to be staring at her granny-panty muffin top. Spanx covers every flaw, allowing women to appear virtually perfect. I have three kids who were all born within a period of three-and-a-half years. Spanx are literally sometimes the only way I can fit into my clothes.

There's something to the idea of smoothing over our flaws, isn't there? As women in the twenty-first century, it has become completely unacceptable to be imperfect. We must all fit like gloves in our designer jeans; we must look put together even when we've "just thrown on" our perfectly color-coordinated fitness gear; we must actually then exercise and be fit; we must be on every PTA board and party-planning committee to show that we are the picture-perfect and uber-involved mom; we must have life-changing ministry oozing from our fingertips…I think you get the picture.

Don't get me wrong. Every woman I know, me included, is quick to point out her shortcomings. The funny thing, though, is that even our shortcomings have been created and then smoothed over to appear "acceptable."

"Oh, I'm just too overcommitted! I keep telling myself that I have to learn to say no to some things, but I always end up scheduling myself crazy," says the mom with a frantic pace of life. (Translation: I'm too busy but also extremely needed.)

"I have got to start back on Weight Watchers. Christmas totally did me in," says the 120-pound mom with a knockout body. (Translation: I let myself eat a slice of pie on Christmas Day.)

"I am not a public speaker; I have no idea why they let me teach a Bible study!" (Translation: I teach a Bible study.)

We allow ourselves to share our inadequacies so that we appear vulnerable; yet our inadequacies are often nothing more than our boastings covered up in humble words…which means we are nowhere near being truly vulnerable. We allow ourselves to appear just imperfect enough to be human, and then we reign it back in and throw some Spanx on our lives so we appear smoothed out in all the right places.

I. Hate. This.

I am looking for real. I am looking for vulnerable. I am looking for messy, for lumpy, for the granny-panty lines in life. I want to shout from the rooftops that you're not, that I'm not, fooling anyone with the so-slightly-imperfect-that-we're-clearly-perfect façades. I want to go deep with women who know me. Not just know *about* me, but know *me*. I want to know them. I want to know that they don't have all their junk together, because I sure don't, and I want to know that we can be messy together.

I am not looking for people who have Spanx for every day of the week. I am looking for people who aren't afraid of LUMPY.

I want to celebrate the things I do right and I want to share the things I do wrong, all in the hope that by doing life in a real way with real women, I will grow. I want to be better. I want to be refined, to look more like Jesus. How can I learn to look more like Him if I pretend that I already do?

I want to be spurred on toward holiness by women who understand what it means to be unholy. I want to run to the foot of the cross with women who understand the desperate need we all have for a merciful, forgiving Savior, a God who meets us where we are and as we are, not as we should be.

Community for Christ-following women must begin with those who are willing to be real.

I'll go first.

I overeat. I shouldn't, but I do, and now I am paying for it with my "~~mid-sized-human~~ brownie weight."

I am prone to gossip. I try to guard my tongue, but there are moments when it just doesn't happen.

I can be super-selfish when it comes to my husband and children. Sometimes I really don't care what they want because all that matters to me in the moment is what I want.

I look for validation from others, and sometimes I perform for their approval instead of God's approval.

And sometimes, even though I know I shouldn't do it, I choose to sin because it feels good and it's fun.

I can go on and on, trust me. I hate these things about myself. Yet I need to share these things with women who care for me so they can know me and so we can walk this Christian life together. We weren't meant to walk alone, but neither were we meant to walk wearing spiritual Spanx.

I love what 1 John 1:5—10 (ESV) says about this:

> *If we say we have fellowship with him while we walk in darkness, we lie and do not practice the truth. But if we walk in the light, as he is in the light, we have fellowship with one another, and the blood of Jesus his Son cleanses us from all sin. If we say we have no sin, we deceive ourselves, and the truth is not in us. If we confess our sins, he is faithful and just to forgive us our sins and to cleanse us from all unrighteousness. If we say we have not sinned, we make him a liar, and his word is not in us.*

These verses are an invitation—no, an admonishment—to grab the nearest pair of scissors and go to town cutting up our spiritual Spanx!

Fellowship, both with our Heavenly Father and with one another—comes from walking in the light. Confessing our brokenness. Sharing our failures. Rejoicing in our weaknesses as reminders of our desperate need for a Savior.

This is the kind of fellowship I need, and these are the kind of women I want to do life with…yet it's so easy to keep others at arm's length so that no one knows what messes we are. But then we're living as prisoners in our own bodies. And then we find we're living lives that aren't real. And then we aren't really known by anyone.

We all long to be known, don't we?

There is good news, friends! We were made to be known by our Creator, our Heavenly Father, who is all-knowing and who knows every single bit of us—even the innermost, nastiest, most broken parts.

> *Oh Lord, you have searched me and known me! You know when I sit down and when I rise up; you discern my thoughts from afar. You search out my path and my lying down and are acquainted with all my ways…Where shall I go from your Spirit? Or where shall I flee from your presence?*

PSALM 139:1–3, 7 (ESV)

There is NO hiding our true selves from Him; He sees it all. This truth would terrify me if it were the end of the story, but praise God, it's not! He doesn't just know us; He actually loves us, in spite of us! Check this out:

> *For while we were still weak, at the right time Christ died for the ungodly. For one will scarcely die for a righteous person—though perhaps for a good person one would dare even to die—but God shows his love for us in that while we were still sinners, Christ died for us.*

ROMANS 5:6–8 (ESV)

Isn't that freeing? Even if we wanted to keep wearing spiritual Spanx forever, it would be impossible to fool Him. And even though He sees our lumps and rolls and dirty and grimy hearts, He loves us fully and without condition. He loves us so much that He sent His Son to die a painful, humiliating death for us—for the bad girls!

God not only made us to be known by Him; He made us to be known by one another! He didn't create us to do life alone, to keep people at arm's length and to carry our burdens, our secrets, and our failures in a secret pouch, all under the façade that we're good girls who have our junk together.

I don't know about you, but I am to the point in my life where I don't have the time or the patience to do halfway relationships with other women. I simply can't do the surface-level thing anymore. If that's what you're looking for in a friend, then keep on walking, 'cause I'm not your girl.

I'm ready to dig deep, to be real, to expose my true self to people who are ready to walk alongside me in my journey toward holiness and wholeness. And I'm ready to walk alongside people who are on the same track.

It's not easy; being real is the hardest thing to do in the face of a culture that applauds perfection. But it's worth it. So I've got my shears, and I'm going to town on my spiritual Spanx, cutting them to shreds.

Will you grab your scissors and join me?

PHONE CALLS FROM PRESCHOOL

"Hi, Mrs. Watts, it's Shannon. Again. Listen, I hate to tell you this, but [insert stifled laughter here] Connor just bit Foster, and it broke the skin. Yes, the same Connor whom Foster bit last week. So, yeah, I don't think Foster is going to be biting again anytime soon. Problem solved!"

—Mrs. Z., preschool teacher and certified saint

VI

Expectations ·

"Always expect the unexpected."

—Someone super-smart

Wax On!

A few years ago, my husband and I were invited to go on a luxury catamaran sailing trip to the British Virgin Islands. For free. I don't mean to rub it in; I just have to mention it because it's the catalyst for the story you're about to read.

As we prepared for our vacation, in the midst of all of the details I was juggling and plans I was making and childcare I was arranging and laundry I was doing, I had an idea.

"Self," I thought, "you should totally go get a bikini wax before the sailing trip. You've always wanted to do it. You're gonna be living in a bathing suit for a week, so, it's really the least you can do for yourself (and everyone else who will be there, for that matter). Besides, how bad can it be?"

(Insert ominous music here.)

Answer? Bad. It can be bad.

I had some time to myself one morning before we left for our trip, so in between errands I pulled in and parked my awesome blue minivan in front of a little store called "Relax and Wax." (Pause for laughter.) The irony of that name never escapes me. There is NOTHING relaxing about what takes place inside that building. It's how they lure you in, though, and it obviously worked for me. Once.

Anyway, at this point I was feeling good about the waxing that was to come. I had been instructed by several friends as to how to get ready before I arrived. I had done a little...er...prep work at home before I went. If you've ever been waxed, you understand. If not, let me explain it by way of allegory: it's necessary to trim the hedges, so to speak, before completely ripping them out of the ground by the root.

I walked in with extreme confidence. I was finally getting my bikini wax. I was a grownup. I could make tough decisions. I could do this.

As I entered, I saw two people sitting at the desk before me. One was a super-attractive Brazilian guy, probably twenty years old. The other was a gorgeous, put-together Brazilian lady who looked like a model.

I got nervous.

"Welcome to Relax and Wax," said the lady in her super-awesome-and-smart-sounding Brazilian accent. "What can I do for you today?"

I paused and looked at the long list of waxing options. I felt overwhelmed.

"Um...I just...uh...just want the regular thing. You know, like, just a bikini wax."

She looked at me closely and asked me if I was waxing for a special occasion. I responded by telling her about our trip, and that, yes, I was waxing in order to not frighten every single person on our boat when wearing my swimsuit. I'm not European. I don't braid my armpit hair. I like smooth sailing, so to speak.

The lady looked at me with condescension, then responded, "Oh, honey, you need better than a bikini wax! You're at Relax and Wax, and we are famous for our Brazilian waxes. It's only five dollars more, and you will love it."

Now, I had walked into the store with my mind already made up about this subject. Bikini wax only; no Brazilian. If you're not familiar with Brazilian waxing, let me again explain this by way of allegory: instead of just weeding and edging your garden, you rip up all the plants.

All. The. Plants.

It was in that moment, for some unknown reason, that I lost my ability to think clearly. I was subject to the sales pitch, and she was good. She went on and on about how much I'd like it and how painless it would be. She guaranteed me that I'd be glad I did it.

So I started to think, "What the heck? For five dollars more, why not try it?"

In hindsight, I can give you a lot of reasons not to try it, reason number one being that it's unbearably painful.

Because she was so authoritative and so incredibly convincing, I agreed to try out the Brazilian specialty. After filling out some quick informational forms and a waiver (uh...there's your sign), I followed the lady, to whom I will henceforth refer as Ms. Miyagi (think *Karate Kid* sensei—wax-on/wax-off dude in female form) back to her booth. She scared me.

As we entered the small room, Ms. Miyagi immediately told me to undress from the waist down and climb up on the exam-type table. I waited for her to leave the room, like they do at the GYN. Then I realized she wasn't going anywhere.

In retrospect, this might have been where the shaming began.

I did as she asked, revealing a pasty-white, pre-summer-tan body that had recently birthed its third child and is was still holding on to an extra forty pounds or so. A sight to behold, to put it mildly. I thought she'd look away while I hoisted myself up onto the exam table.

No.

She wasn't staring in a creepy kind of way, but more in an I-do-this-all-day-long-so-just-get-on-the-dang-table-so-I-can-get-this-over-with kind of way.

I was thinking sort of the opposite, the whole "I-don't-normally-get-undressed-then-climb-awkwardly-onto-a-tall-table-in-front-of-people" thought.

But climb I did, with a lot of simultaneous huffing and grunting.

Ms. Miyagi didn't speak a lot. She went right to work and began covering me in hot wax—and yes, I mean HOT wax. I kind of jumped at the first swipe, as she gave me the evil eye. I told myself to man up, that it wouldn't be that bad, that women do this all the time, and all that self-pep talk. She continued to lather, and then she explained to me that once the wax dried, she would remove it.

"Remove" is a funny word. It sounds fairly innocuous to me, even gentle, like you remove the pot from the stove or you remove your shoes. Easy peasy, right?

Wrong.

When she determined that the first strip of wax had hardened, she told me to breathe in. I should have known that anything that required me to pace my breathing was going to be awful, but obediently I breathed in and then out slowly. As I breathed out, Ms. Miyagi yanked that strip of wax off my inner thigh so hard and so fast that I screamed and shot straight up off the table like Br'er Rabbit when he hit the briar patch.

This is something, for future reference, that you never want to do while getting a Brazilian wax. You see, when one screams and shoots straight up off the exam table, one clenches one's legs together, and the still-warm wax that is covering the other inner thigh area immediately transfers to the whole region.

Ms. Miyagi looked at me, disgusted.

"NO," she told me loudly, irritated beyond belief. "You NEVER move during a Brazilian wax."

Humiliated, I quickly understood why. After I lay back down, I realized that my left inner thigh was now stuck to my right inner thigh and that I was a hard, waxy mess.

#Uh-Oh

Over the next thirty minutes, through the use of a mixture of hot water, tweezers, and latex gloves (for her benefit), Ms. Miyagi picked off every fleck of dry, hardened wax acting as glue to my pelvic region. She was, understandably, not happy. She had only successfully waxed one section of my body, and she was a solid forty minutes into the process. My feeble attempts at an apology didn't seem to help much, either.

Once the wax was peeled and picked, she prepared the hot wax for the next section. At this point, I was seriously contemplating cutting my losses, getting dressed, and getting the heck outta Dodge, because I didn't know if I could handle feeling such intense pain again. (I've had three kids; childbirth was a breeze compared to getting waxed—and that's no lie.)

I told her I might just head out, and she shook her head at me. "You will finish," said Ms. Miyagi. "You felt the worst part and it won't be that bad again."

#Lies

I did, however, force myself to remain still and calm as the waxing continued, even though I was crying inside.

It was at the 50-minute mark that Ms. Miyagi announced that she was finished. My feeling of relief was almost tangible. I was breathing hard; my body was pouring sweat. My mascara had smeared down my face from the tears that had welled up in my eyes. I felt giddy and proud, though, now that she had finished, like I had earned a badge of honor

Then she told me to turn over

It was this part of the Brazilian waxing process that I was unaware of. I looked at her and simply asked, "Huh?"

"Turn over; we must finish," instructed Ms. Miyagi

Against my better judgment, I did what she said…because I was superscared of her at this point.

"Uh, why am I doing this, exactly?" I asked Ms. Miyagi

"So I can wax your rear end," she said, as though I were a complete idiot, which obviously I was

I soaked in what she said.

"Oh, no, that's okay, I don't need anything else waxed, thank you very much," I stuttered and stammered, as Ms. Miyagi stirred her evil wax

"Honey," she responded calmly in her Brazilian-accented voice, "EVERYONE needs a full wax, and we're going to finish it. We're almost done."

Again, falling prey to her power and authority, I shut my mouth, rolled over, and came to terms with the fact that this was, indeed, happening.

She quietly prepared her wax. In retrospect, I should have stopped. I should've hopped down from that crazy lady's table and run for the door.

Instead I waited, on all fours and anxiety-ridden, for her to apply the last bit of wax. It was at that very moment that "the incident" occurred.

"Brrrrrrrrrrrrrrrrrrrrrrrrrrt."

That was the sound the air made as it unexpectedly escaped from my body.

I'll give you a minute to soak that in.

Are you back with me? Okay. So, yes, in answer to your first and obvious question, I did indeed pass gas right there on the waxing table. Out loud. In the silent, sterile room.

I would like to point out that Ms. Miyagi was really the one responsible for this occurrence. I am also convinced there must be scientific proof that one has at least a 50/50 chance of a methane-induced incident occurring during a Brazilian wax when one assumes strange positions like this.

So, yes, it happened. Then, silence

I decided that the mature thing to do would be to broach the subject first, seeing as how I was the offender in the situation.

"Um, I'm pretty sure I just tooted on your table," I told Ms. Miyagi

She continued working. "Yes."

That's all. Not, "Don't worry about it," or, "It happens." Just, "Yes."

At this point, all I could think about was how fast I could get from the waxing room to my car. She finished lathering the wax, and the pain I felt when she ripped it off was nothing compared to the pain in my heart from the anxiety-induced palpitations I was experiencing

"Done," said Ms. Miyagi, closing her vat of wax and tossing her medical gloves in the trash can.

"Thank you," I said meekly, as she walked out the door without another word.

Left alone and ashamed, I quickly threw my clothes back on, paying no attention to the fact that the little bits of wax left on my nether regions were causing my underwear to stick awkwardly to my body. I grabbed my purse and went out to the front desk to pay

When I got to the desk, Ms. Miyagi was sitting with Mr. Young Brazilian Stud Muffin, speaking to him in Portuguese and laughing hysterically

I wonder what she was telling him

Humiliated, and knowing Mr. Good-Looking was picturing me blowing it out on the waxing table, I threw a wad of cash at Ms. Miyagi and hightailed it for the door. I ran to my car, and did the only thing I knew to do, which was to convulse in nervous laughter.

I called my husband, hysterical, because I had to, as we say in the church world, "unpack" what had just happened to me.

He was silent. I'm sure it was because it was such an attractive mental picture for him and because he was so proud, in that moment, to be my husband I drove away from Relax and Wax anything but relaxed and vowing never, NEVER to subject myself to that pain and humiliation again. And I haven't. I haven't gone back. Maybe one day I'll get up the nerve to try again—at some other waxing salon, of course. Maybe not. Probably not.

At this point, you're probably wondering how I'm going to tie this in to a spiritual truth, aren't you? You're thinking that it's just not possible. Well, read and be amazed.

If there's one thing we learn in life, it is that we should always expect the unexpected. Even if the unexpected sounds like, "Brrrrrrrrrrrrrrrrrrrrrrrrrt."

Life is not always—not usually—going to happen as we expect. Our plans aren't God's plans. We can't see the big picture the way He sees the big picture. We can set our expectations and make big plans and still see life change on a dime

Sometimes life's funny or embarrassing, like my unfortunate incident at Relax and Wax. Sometimes its unexpected turns are painful and hard, like when my sweet friend had to say goodbye to her too-young-to-die husband and father of their three children after a hard-fought battle with cancer. Sometimes we face unexpected financial loss, like the day a sixty-year-old man finds out that his job is being eliminated.

We have to expect the unexpected.

However, and this is important, we don't have to FEAR the unexpected. Do you know why?

Because there is a very real, completely sovereign God who knows and loves us, and nothing is unexpected to Him.

The definition of "sovereign" is this: "Being above all others in character, knowledge, and excellence."

Sovereign. This perfectly sums up both who God is and who we are not. Scripture makes it clear that He alone knows and sees the big picture:

The heart of man plans his way,
but the Lord establishes his steps.

PROVERBS 16:9 (ESV)

The Lord reigns, He is clothed with majesty; the Lord has
clothed and girded Himself with strength. Indeed, the world
is firmly established; it will not be moved.

PSALM 93:1 (ESV)

Because of God's sovereignty, when we believe Him to be who He says He is, fear no longer need have a hold on us because, as it says in Matthew:

What's the price of a pet canary? Some loose change, right?
And God cares what happens to it even more than you do.
He pays even greater attention to you, down to the last
detail—even numbering the hairs on your head!

MATTHEW 10:29–30 (MSG)

He cares. He loves us. And He sees the big picture. Nothing catches Him off guard, not even a Brazilian wax gone very, very wrong. So be encouraged. He will not fail you.

It's time for me to wrap this story up. After writing about it, I feel like I have relived some of the trauma I experienced at Relax and Wax. I think I need a massage. Maybe I'll schedule one at the spa here on the cruise ship as a treat. Nothing bad could POSSIBLY come of a massage…could it?

Shattered Expectations

Have you ever had one of those completely magical, seemingly perfect, carefree days with your kids, the kind that you never want to end and that feels completely utopian in every single way?

Me neither.

Honestly, I really haven't. Don't get me wrong—we've had great times; idyllic experiences, even. But, and this is a big BUT, the picture perfection never lasts all day long. I think it's literally impossible to make it through an entire day without dysfunction, because my house is full of a bunch of sinners. Big sinners and little sinners, old and young. Sinners with perfect pitch and those who are tone-deaf. (Yes, my children appear to be tone-deaf. Maybe they'll outgrow it.)

I've learned to adjust my expectations and to expect conflict and frustration and stress. If I don't expect these things, I know I'll be sorely let down again and again and again, as previously illustrated in the waxing debacle.

If I didn't already know this, I recently had an experience that shattered any illusion I may have had of having the perfect day once and for all. I don't mean to share this in a woe-is-me kind of way; it's not like that at all. It's just my reality, and it's actually refreshing, because it's yet another reminder that all of you "Graces" out there in social media world who like to create the illusion of perfection in your homes are L-I-A-R-S. (In case you're just finding this out, the whole world knows that your kids are little sinners, too.)

It was day four of Daddy being out of town and day 9,778 (or so it seemed) of constant rain. Softball? Cancelled. T-ball? Cancelled? Outdoor play options? Nada. Three stir-crazy, full-of-energy kiddos who were bouncing off the walls? Roger that.

I tried my best to give them an outlet for their energy. I took them in the morning to an indoor play place, where I paid $31.79 (yes, that is DOLLARS…at a germ-infested jungle gym…by my OWN CHOOSING) for them to play for an hour. I then had to pack everyone up to leave because my middle child was "tired" and wanted to "go home" and started to have an emotional breakdown. Miraculously, he perked right up and started building Legos as soon as we got home.

I made it through a rainy afternoon, surviving solely based on the knowledge that, come 5:00 p.m., my babysitter was coming to take over, and I was going out. Alone.

I showered (maybe for the first time in four days), got ready, and hit the road faster than Wiley Coyote chasing the Roadrunner.

"See ya! Don't call me unless someone's bleeding," was pretty much the extent of my instructions.

Disclaimer: I love my kids, I really do. And the insecure part of me hesitates to write as honestly as I do for fear that people will think I'm a bad mom who is constantly irritated by her kids. That's not true; I'm actually a great mom who is constantly irritated by her kids. Because kids are irritating. And awesome. And I love them.

#JustClearingThatUp

I had a great night out. Did a little shopping. Met a friend for dinner. We even sat in the restaurant long after we were done with our meal and talked without interruption (I know, right?). It was such a nice reprieve.

Then I came home.

Here's the part of the story where I encourage you to grab a bowl of popcorn and settle in, 'cause this is one of those "these-things-only-happen-to-Jordan"-type things.

I opened the front door (at this point, is was close to 10:00 p.m.), expecting quiet and calmness. Instead, I heard the TV blaring and my three-year-old talking loudly.

#Awesome

As I walked into the front entryway, I quickly noticed that my rug was covered in popcorn kernels. Not popped popcorn, but the whole kernels.

#Interesting

I ventured ahead into the living room, where I found popped popcorn strewed wall to wall, along with two kids' cups knocked on their sides and slowly leaking onto my fairly new rug. The rug that the kids aren't allowed to eat or drink on.

#Perturbed

I backtracked and made the turn into the kitchen. There I found a half-eaten pizza on the counter, its top picked completely clean of cheese and pepperoni. Basically, I was left with half a slab of bread with tomato sauce on it for leftovers.

#Yummy

All over the kitchen counter and floor were more popcorn kernels. Hundreds. I've found them for months, like tiny little painful surprises for the soles of my feet that keep on coming...and coming...and coming.

#Ouch

At this point, I called out to the babysitter who, I discovered, was with my three-year-old in another room. She walked into the kitchen.

"How'd it go tonight?" I asked.

"It was a rough one," she answered.

#YaThink?

She explained to me that everything had been going well, that the kids had played and eaten and then wanted to watch a movie. She attempted to pop popcorn in our hot-air popcorn machine and overfilled it, causing it to smoke and burn. In an attempt to get that situation under control, the bottle of popcorn kernels accidentally got knocked off the counter and spilled everywhere. Literally everywhere. As in, the next morning, in my bedroom at the other end of the house, the first thing my foot touched when I rolled out of bed was a popcorn kernel.

#GoodMorning

She ended up getting the popcorn sitch happening, so the kids sat and ate popcorn and watched a movie in the living room...on the rug. So that explained that.

Then came, as Oprah likes to call it, the "AHA moment" for me. My sitter explained that, because the kids had been SO well behaved, she gave them a treat. A candy treat, to be more specific. Right before bedtime.

They discovered a bag of gummy worms in our kitchen cabinet. These gummy worms were, in actuality, for my seven-year-old's Earth Day class project the next week. However, upon finding the Trolli Sour Brite

Crawlers, my three children proceeded to eat every last one of them (under the sitter's supervision). The. Entire. One-Pound. Bag.

#Aha!

Apparently, that's when everything went south (as though that had not already happened). The kids got amped up on an enormous sugar high and couldn't be calmed down for bed. They discovered Silly Putty and green Play-Doh in the kitchen cabinet and started running through the house, throwing it at each other and acting stupid. There was evidence of this stupidity on my walls. And on my floors. And on my new living room rug. And on the 60-inch flat-screen TV that they broke when they threw a big ball of Silly Putty through the living room, smashing it into the television.

#IWishIWereKidding

Yes, that's right, ladies and gentlemen. They broke our flat-screen TV.

#Cuss

#CussAgain

After all of this went down, the sitter somehow got my older two ~~sinners~~ kids to bed; then she attempted to get my youngest down. He refused. I guess she accepted that refusal. And so that is how I found him watching TV when I returned home at 10:00 p.m.

To give my sitter credit, she had been so busy corralling the troops that she hadn't had time to clean up a single thing. To give my kids some credit, my sitter had thought it was a good idea to give them an entire bag of gummy worms moments before bedtime. And then she expected them to calmly and quietly go to sleep without a fight.

In the words of George H. W., "NOT GONNA HAPPEN!"

I got #3 tucked into bed and started the cleanup process. And what a process it was! Sweeping. Vacuuming. Peeling Silly Putty and Play-Doh out of my rug and off my floors and off my walls and off my kitchen cutting boards (I don't even get that one). Cleaning up liquid spills and popcorn kernels and actual popcorn and cold pizza: just what every mom wants to do at the end of a night out, am I right?

#Wrong

I started out feeling surprised upon arriving at home. Then I grew frustrated. Then annoyed. Then angry.

And then I laughed.

#FeelFreeToLaughWithMe

I realized, in that moment as I sat down in my favorite armchair and surveyed my now-cleaned-up house, that life is all about expectations and reality.

I had expected to come home to a quiet, clean house after a long week of single parenting, and I didn't get what I expected (methinks it wasn't the evening my babysitter expected, either). My expectations can make or break virtually any situation that comes my way, and I'm guessing yours can, too.

When we hold others (or ourselves, for that matter) to the impossible standard of perfection, we will be disappointed over and over again. When we want life to fall into place in a picture-perfect way, and we expect nothing less than that, we are bound for frustration and disillusionment.

The worst part, I think, is that when life isn't idyllic or when people let us down or we fail ourselves, we project that imperfection onto God Himself. I've done it before, and so have you.

When our circumstances are dire and we see no light at the end of the tunnel and we're disappointed because we expected God to change our situations and save us from the pain and misery we're experiencing, it's easy to decide that God is a fraud. That He's not who He says He is. That He doesn't care.

When people mistreat us and let us down and wound us to our cores, it's easy to decide that no one is worth trusting.

When we let ourselves down and give in to sin and darkness even though we know better, it's easy to decide that we are ourselves the definition of failure and that we deserve for shame to name and define us.

If our expectations are perfection—or even just basic goodness—we will be let down time and time again, mainly because humankind is a hot mess.

However, the grace of God covers all of our imperfections…and His perfection is the best gap-filler. When life disappoints us, He is perfect and in control. When people disappoint us, He is our friend and our Father who picks up the slack. When we disappoint ourselves and loathe our own reflections, He shows us our new faces and reminds us of our new names, found in the person of Jesus Christ.

We must expect the world to fail us, and we must cling to the truth that God never will.

> *This God—His way is perfect; the word of the Lord proves true; He is a shield for all those who take refuge in Him. For who is God but the Lord? And who is a rock except our God?*
> Psalm *18:30–31 (ESV)*

If we do this, our expectations will no longer be rooted in fanciful illusions but will instead be rooted in He Who Never Changes and Never Fails. Disappointment will be no more because He is always good and, as it says in Psalm 52:8b (ESV), we can fully and evermore "trust in the steadfast love of God forever and ever."

I know I can trust Him. As for my children or my babysitter...well, the jury's still out on that. For now, we'll just have to be creative.

"Mom, why didn't God make you as pretty as me?"

—*A friend's daughter during cuddle time*

VII

Feelings

"I'm in a glass case of emotion!"

—Ron Burgundy

Satan Is A Liar

Brace yourselves, people: I'm putting on my therapist hat. You know, the one that I have no training or authority to wear? That being said, I will rock this hat like Pharrell Williams.

Let's talk about feelings. My feelings. Yours, too. Because I know I'm not the only one who feels things.

I can say with complete certainty that there are other people who feel things besides yours truly. This is because one of these people lives in my home.

My daughter. The feelings. The hormones. Oy vey.

Since she was eighteen months old, I have said—often with sincere concern—that the time of the weeping womb is upon her. Sometimes I honestly think Aunt Flow is coming to visit her at age eight due to the indescribable emotions that seep from her very core.

Don't get me wrong; she is a wonderfully delightful tiny human. But when she feels...well, she feels, if you get my drift.

I remember one incident that occurred when she was around four years old. She and her brother were together and, as usual, they were playing really well until they weren't anymore. My son ran into the house to find me, weeping because his sister had pushed him down.

Now, in our house, using your hands to hurt someone else is an automatic trip to the penalty box. So naturally, I found my (unrepentant) daughter and asked her to go sit on her bed for five minutes and think about the way she had treated her brother and how she should do it differently next time. Off she ran to her room, and what followed was nothing short of an Oscar-worthy performance.

First I heard the weeping. Then the wailing. It started as a faint whimper, but the volume steadily rose in order, no doubt, to gain my attention. And that it did. How could it not? I think the neighbors at the end of the cul-de-sac could probably hear what was happening in the Watts house.

Next came the self-deprecating remarks.

"Waaaaaaaaahhhhhhhhhhh! Why am I so naughty? Waaaaaaaahhhhhhhhh!"

"MommyMommyMommyMommyMommy, I am so unkiiiiiiinnnnddd!"

"Ooooohhhhhhh, I am the baddest person in this familyyyyyy! Waaaahhhhh!"

I wish I were making this up. But then it wouldn't have happened and I wouldn't be writing this embarrassing story with which I will surely hold my daughter hostage in her teenage years, pulling out a copy of this book to show prospective boyfriends so they know ahead of time just what they're dabbling in. (Really, it's just my mama-bear way of trying to ensure she doesn't date until she's twenty-five.)

Next came my favorite part, my favorite mainly because it displayed her creativity in such a powerful way. She began some pretty angst-y stream-of-consciousness songwriting. The kind that would make Alanis Morissette proud. Her song went a little something like this:

"Why...does nobody love me?
"Why...does nobody care for me?
"Why...does nobody want me in their family?
"Whyyyyyyyyyy?"

(PAUSE)

"Emerson, I love you.
"I think you're great
"And so kind and beautiful,
"And you have beautiful hair.
"I am GODDDDDDDDDDD!"

At least she doesn't suffer from low self-esteem.

This example is the tip of the proverbial iceberg, to be sure. The emotions definitely flow freely with that chick, and while it can be entertaining and even frustrating at times, there is something appealing about watching her feel things.

There can be a problem, though, with feelings. It's far too easy for us to allow our feelings to color our perceived realities; in other words, I feel; therefore, it must be true.

See the above example concerning my daughter: she was disciplined (fairly and in love), and she allowed her feelings to distort reality. Did we no longer love her or care for her or want her in our family because she shoved her little brother? Absolutely not. However, in those moments, her feelings overtook what she knew to be true, and she allowed the lies of the enemy to rule her mind.

Oftentimes, feelings do not accurately represent reality.

It's a lot like this with God and me. When things are good and I feel positive emotions, I believe that He loves me and has my best interests in mind. I say, "Thank you, Lord, for your blessings," and, "You are faithful and good," and things of that nature.

It's when life gets stormy that the doubt starts to creep in. And in the storms, the worst thing I can do is to trust my feelings.

#CanIGetAWitness?

All of us feel, and we feel a lot. The question is how do we reconcile our feelings with our faith in God's sovereignty and His bigger plan? How do we learn to trust that He has our best interests in mind when it feels like He is absent, that He just doesn't care? How do we keep our feelings from dictating what is truth and what is not?

I think the answer is simple:

TRUTH TRUMPS FEELINGS.

Every. Single. Time.

God's Word mentions "truth" over 230 times. We know this is not by accident. I believe it's because sometimes I am so dense that God needs to repeat Himself countless times to make sure I get what He's saying.

He knows our feelings will come and overtake us, that they'll threaten to rule us; He knows that we are easily swayed. This is why He has given his Spirit of truth to each and every one of His children. I love the words that Jesus spoke, recorded in the book of John, because He knew that, although He was going away, God was going to leave us a guide and protector:

> *When the Spirit of truth comes, he will guide you into*
> *all truth, for he will not speak on his own authority, but*
> *whatever he hears he will speak, and he will declare to you*
> *the things that are to come. He will glorify me, for he will*
> *take what is mine and declare it to you.*

> JOHN 16:13–14 (ESV)

We must continually measure our feelings against God's truth. He has given us the Spirit of truth and His Word as fantastic litmus tests. If our emotions can't stand up against the truth of who He is, we must choose to replace our feelings—the lies—with His truth. Easier said than done, I know, but it's something to strive for, isn't it?

Over the last eighteen months, my family has experienced a handful of hardships. My cousin (age 32) was rushed into emergency surgery due to kidney malfunction. Another cousin (age 20) was in a horrific waterskiing accident, resulting in a broken back and fractured skull. It's amazing that he's alive, honestly. Yet another cousin (age 22) was diagnosed with thyroid cancer. My great aunt was diagnosed with, and quickly passed away from, cancer. My father experienced job loss and financial stresses. My mother has dealt with debilitating back pain. My parents' marriage almost collapsed. I'm not going to lie—it's been a lot to process. There have been a lot of feelings welling up in me.

There have been moments when I've been tempted to question God's goodness and faithfulness, when I've doubted His ability to handle all that is going on in the life of my family. There have been times when I've been close to allowing fear to consume me, when I've been on the edge of thinking that maybe my Heavenly Father is absent or not who He claims to be. There have been times when I haven't felt like He is near, times when I haven't felt confident in His sovereignty.

Thank goodness I don't rely on my feelings.

John Piper says it so much better than I do:

> *My feelings are not God. God is God. My feelings do not define truth. God's word defines truth. My feelings are echoes and responses to what my mind perceives. And sometimes— many times—my feelings are out of sync with the truth. When that happens—and it happens every day in some measure—I try not to bend the truth to justify my imperfect feelings, but rather, I plead with God: Purify my perceptions*

of [your] truth and transform my feelings so that they are in
sync with the truth.[ii]

Pleading with God is more than just asking. "Pleading" signifies desperation. In a world where our enemy, Satan, wants to feed us lies, and as a weak and broken people who are susceptible to fall for those lies, let's plead with God, begging him to "purify our perceptions of [His] truth and transform [our] feelings so that they are in sync with the truth!"

If it helps you to center your mind on truth, feel free to follow my daughter's example and put pen to paper as you talk with God. Maybe He'll answer back and tell you how pretty your hair is in the process.

Pain Intolerance

I recently read a Facebook post by a friend that detailed the fifty-seven tasks that she had checked off her to-do list that day, along with a picture of her little ones all cuddled up together on the sofa, holding each other lovingly before bedtime.

I was like, "Um, yeah, so today I kept the kids alive, let them watch entirely too much TV, and didn't even get my one load of laundry folded. BOOM."

#DropTheMic

No, I'm not that lazy (usually). I had awakened that morning from what was a terrible night's sleep to one of the worst pinched nerves in my neck that I have ever experienced. Ever. My sweet husband had to come home early from work and take over kid duty for the remainder of the day because I could not move.

Pain can be all-consuming, can't it? It's pretty amazing, if you think about it, how pain, even a small amount, can vie for our attention. We never think of how good it feels to feel…well…good until we feel pain. And when we do, all we can think about is alleviating said pain and getting back to normal.

I remember being in the throes of a crazy, chaotic day a few years ago. I was taking my two-year-old from the pediatrician's office to the hospital for some blood tests (that's always scary) when, in my hurry, I accidentally slammed my index finger in the car door.

Now, this wasn't just an "ow" kind of a moment. This was an "I-have-to-reach-over-with-my-other-hand-and-open-the-car-door-to-get-my-finger-out-because-it's-actually-closed-in-there" moment. Within seconds, the nerves in my finger registered with my brain, and I am pretty sure I said a few inappropriate things while I fell on the ground of the parking garage, writhing around in pain.

Finally, I jumped up and got in the car and set out for the hospital. By the time we arrived there, my fingernail was completely black, and my finger was so swollen that I couldn't bend it. You know it's bad when the staff at the local children's hospital is more concerned about you, the parent, than they are about your child, who is actually the patient.

By the end of the afternoon, my finger hurt so badly that I thought I was going to die. I finally decided to go to the nearby urgent care facility in the hope that they could help me. Help me, they did. After an x-ray to ensure that I hadn't fractured the bone (which I hadn't), the doctor said he could help me by relieving the pressure caused by all the blood that was pooled under my fingernail. "All" I had to do was sit still and allow him to use a little heat wand to burn a hole in my fingernail, thus allowing the blood to escape.

It was about as fun as it sounds.

When we are in intense physical pain, though, there's really nothing we wouldn't do to feel relief, is there? In actuality, we run from pain. We have our remedies and medicines and holistic approaches down pat, all to find escape from the pain (I should own stock in ibuprofen, because that stuff is the business when it comes to pain management).

But what about when our souls ache? What about when our hearts break?

No one likes to feel pain. But I think that even the biggest wimp would admit that physical pain is often easier to endure than emotional, heart-ravaging hurt. We try to build walls to keep others out of our pain because it's too tender a subject to broach with them. We pretend like we don't hurt. We numb our pain in many different ways. We stuff our feelings and the things that are uncomfortable to think about under the rug, and we move in and out of our daily routines like nothing has changed.

I have a novel idea, one that is easy to say but extremely difficult to do: what if, when our hearts hurt, instead of trying to escape the pain and the hurt, we embrace it and allow it to transform our very beings? What if the pain actually points us to Him—and what if we miss Him when we hide our pain? What if bearing the load of heartache is part of what it means in Scripture when Paul writes about knowing, truly knowing Christ, by sharing in the fellowship of His sufferings (Philippians 3:10)?

What if, when friends or loved ones hurt us, we process through the pain and allow the Lord to change our character and refine us in the process, making us look more like Jesus? What if, instead of hiding our shame and our sin, we shine light on it and live transparent lives that, while messy and sometimes sad, point people to their need for a gracious, loving God?

What if we don't sit idly by as we see injustice around us, injustice that wrecks our hearts? What if, instead of just being sad because of the AIDS epidemic in Africa and finding ways to distract our minds from having to dwell on such a depressing issue, we embrace the sadness and allow it to ignite in us a passion to do something? What if, instead of feeling sad that my own city, the city of Atlanta, Georgia, is the largest haven for sex traffickers in the world and trying not to think about it because it disturbs my "happy" reality, I allow it to penetrate the thick walls I've built around my heart and realize, "I am NOT okay with this." I'm preaching to myself here!

What if the only way to wholly heal our hearts is to embrace our pain and allow our Heavenly Father to break us down so that we might be rebuilt into versions of ourselves that look an awful lot more like Jesus?

One of my favorite worship tunes of all time is a song by Hillsong United called "Hosanna." The bridge of the song is the cry of my heart, and I pray that we wouldn't miss this:

Heal my heart and make it clean
Open up my eyes to the things unseen
Show me how to love like You have loved me
Break my heart for what breaks Yours
Everything I am for Your kingdom's cause
As I walk from earth into eternity[iii]

Healing my heart often means that God must break my heart first. Am I okay with that? Are you?

What if instead of living our perfectly scripted lives as perfect little Christians, we allowed the ugly and the messy out, and we decided to live like Jesus? What if we were to actually DO something about the things that break our hearts? Do you think the world would look different?

I do.

If you'd like to dig more into this, if the Lord's moving in your heart, I'd encourage you to grab yourself a copy of *Radical* by David Platt. If you're someone who isn't satisfied with the status quo, if you feel like there's something more to following Christ than drive-through Sunday morning church services and the occasional daily devotional, read this book. Soak it in. And let me know what you think.

It's time for us to allow ourselves to feel in order that we might be changed. Then our families will be changed. Then our communities. Then our country. Then the world.

<u>STUFF MY KIDS SAY</u>

"You know how you get Jesus in your heart?
You throw a big stick real far and then see if He catches it."

—*Sutton Watts, age 3*

VIII

Faith

"True faith means holding nothing back. It means putting every hope in God's fidelity to His promises."

—FRANCIS CHAN, *Crazy Love: Overwhelmed by a Relentless God*

Gristina

I think I should be paid in mom bucks for every question I answer each day. If one mom buck equals sixty seconds of alone time, I am fairly confident that I would earn, on average, 987 blissful minutes to myself every afternoon.

Kids want to know "why." We know this to be true—no debate necessary. My kids question everything, and then some.

There are some questions kids only seem to ask in public places within earshot of some easily offended old lady or some grumpy-and-having-a-bad-day man-child who can't afford to share a smile, even with the cutest children in the world (mine).

Things my kids have asked in public places:

"Mommy, did you tooter again?"
(Insinuating that I had done it once already.)

"Does she have a baby in her belly?"
(Answer: that's what we refer to as a "food baby.")

"Hey, man, why do you talk like such a girl?"
(To the effeminate guy checking us out at the grocery store.)

"How did I get in your belly?"
(Crickets…)

"Where's your legs is?"
(Question asked to the double amputee in the lobby of our pediatrician's office.)

"Why does Daddy have hair on his tail?"
(There's so much to dig through here, I just don't know where to begin.)

"Why does your arm shake like jello when I poke it?"
(Answer: because I wrecked my body for you, my angel.)

"How do we go to heaven and live with God?"
(Asked by my three-year-old, whom I answered with my sage wisdom.)

He then followed up that question with:

"When I get there, is God gonna ask me why I don't have pants on and my private parts are showing?"
(*Sigh*)

Kids can also ask tough questions, the kind of questions that immediately make parents start to sweat and pray silently for fear of giving the wrong answer:

"How is God everywhere?"

"Why does God let people go hungry when He can make food appear by saying a word?"

"Why didn't God heal ____?"

"How did Noah get two of every kind of animal on the earth in one boat?"

"What does God look like?"

"Who made God?"

"Will you know I'm your daughter when we're in heaven?"

These are the kinds of questions that send parents running for the hills, so to speak...the kinds of questions that are easier to simply not answer and discuss, the kinds of questions children ask without reservation.

As adults, we have lost our nerve a bit. Asking questions makes us (and often others) uncomfortable. We're afraid we might sound uneducated. We worry that we might stir the pot and draw attention to ourselves. We might be anxious that we won't like the answers we find. For those of us who walk with God, we're afraid that questions equal unbelief and that it's unacceptable to ask our questions for fear we might reveal our hidden doubts.

I have this friend who questions everything. Let's say her name rhymes with "Gristina." She's a cynic. She picks issues apart until she has dissected them to her satisfaction. She chews slowly on things and will continue to chew, sometimes for long periods of time, examining her belief system, her theology, and the Word of God.

I respect her so much.

Sometimes she drives herself crazy. Sometimes she gets so much into her own head that she feels trapped. Sometimes she questions and doubts and, instead of accepting a rote answer as truth, she digs and digs and thinks and thinks. Then she prays and thinks some more. She absolutely refuses to settle for a "just because" answer.

And that is the hard path. It can be lonely and dark, especially in a world where many accept the easiest-to-swallow answers, the truth that makes them feel good so they can have a semblance of peace and move on to the next item on their to-do lists.

But.

It's in the poking and the prodding, in the questioning and in the dissecting where we truly learn to own our own faith. When we are spoon-fed the answers, believing them as truth—just as little children accept as fact whatever they're told—our faith has a tendency to be shallow, void of conviction and confidence.

This friend and I, we used to be in a Bible study together. She would always ask questions and she didn't shy away from controversy. It's inspiring, really. She voiced her opinions and challenged people on theirs when she felt that they were not lining up with truth. She did this with grace and humility, and she spurred on the rest of us to examine what we truly believed about various topics.

She can be a bit of a pessimist, and she loves to play the devil's advocate. And she is fabulous.

She knows that not all of her questions can be answered on this side of eternity. And she accepts this and walks in faith, trusting God. But it doesn't stop her from asking the questions. Because who is God if we can't come to Him as a child comes to his parent with the questions of life? And who is God if He's not personal enough to allow us to sit in His presence, expressing our hurts and our pains and our doubts and our frustrations?

If we couldn't come to the Lord with honesty, it would make Him an impersonal deity who lacks mercy for His fallen creation. And we know that our Heavenly Father is far from that kind of God.

God made us and knows us by name. He can count the hairs on my head. And your head. And her head. And so on. Shouldn't we feel the freedom to come to Him with our confusion and doubts? To ask the hard questions, because we know that He can handle our lack of understanding and that He loves us so deeply that He desires for us to know Him fully, at least as fully as we possibly can while separated from Him in this screwed-up world?

So I think we question, we dig. But we do it while tempering our curiosity and our frustrations with this truth: we are, simply, not going to have full understanding and all of the answers while we are a broken people in a broken world.

Paul says is best, I think, in his letter to the church at Corinth:

> *We don't yet see things clearly. We're squinting in a fog,*
> *peering through a mist. But it won't be long before the*
> *weather clears and the sun shines bright! We'll see it all then,*
> *see it all as clearly as God sees us, knowing him directly just*
> *as he knows us!*

1 CORINTHIANS 13:12 (MSG)

And at the end of the day, when we are stuck in a place of confusion and we lack understanding and everything in us wants to just create a "happy" answer to our questions about God so that we feel better and can wrap up our issues in pretty paper with a great big bow, we must remember that when we are at an impasse with God...HE WINS. He must always win. We must look off into the distance and remember that we are not home yet. And home is where our Father awaits us to wholly answer our questions.

> *It's impossible to please God apart from faith. And why?*
> *Because anyone who wants to approach God must believe*
> *both that he exists and that he cares enough to respond to*
> *those who seek him...Each one of these people of faith [Abel,*
> *Enoch, Noah, Abraham, Sarah] died not yet having in hand*
> *what was promised, but still believing. How did they do it?*
> *They saw it way off in the distance, waved their greeting,*

and accepted the fact that they were transients in this world.
People who live this way make it plain that they are looking
for their true home.

HEBREWS 11:1–16, PARAPHRASED

This, my friends, in a nutshell, is walking with God. Trying our best to discern what is right and true, using the tools He has given us (i.e., the Word of God, the Holy Spirit, wise counsel, etc.), while ultimately resting in the fact that we are not going to have complete understanding until we are made complete on the other side of eternity.

In the meantime, if you're a chew-on-the-question kind of person and you want to help me answer some of the 987 questions I am asked each and every day by my inquisitive children, holla back and help a sister out. If you'd start by trying to answer my son's most recent question, that'd be rad: "Mom, is that a man or a woman?"

Gucky Broccoli

My youngest child, Foster, was somewhat of a late bloomer. As is often typical for a third child, he crawled late, walked late, and talked late. For a while there, I was starting to ~~hope~~ think he'd NEVER talk (call me Mother of the Year, but that would not necessarily have been a bad thing, since my other two got in a total of about 50,000 words each day).

Don't you worry (in case you were worried). When Foster reached his second birthday, along with the various tractors and other loud boy-toys he was given, I think he must have also received his big-boy britches. The words started flowing, the attitude kicked into high gear, and he decided he was ready to roll with the big dogs.

He added many new words to his vocabulary, which had previously consisted of "Daddy," "Mommy," and "no." Words like: gucky (yucky), peeya (pizza or his man parts, depending on the situation), teet (treat), and more.

He also discovered the power of a shrill, glass-shattering scream which, when loosed around his brother or sister, immediately beckoned the adult of the house. Said adult would then come running while chiding, "Who hurt Foster?" I only recently realized that, in fact, Foster had probably assaulted one of his siblings instead of the other way around, and that screaming and getting them in trouble for something he had done was like the cherry on top of the ice cream sundae for him. He was living large and keeping our home...lively.

He was learning to work the system. I quickly realized how much I babied him. I began to see that he was a lot smarter than I had previously given him credit for and that Brandon and I really needed to make an effort to stop coddling him and start treating him like the little sinner toddler he was.

All of this background info is to set the scene so that you will have a greater understanding of what went down one night when Foster was a little over two years old. It was epic.

On this particular evening after a LONG week of home renovation work (that we did ourselves), we sat down to dinner in a just-put-back-together house, breathing a sigh of relief. It had been crazy around the Watts house, and after spending much of the day cleaning, I finally felt sane again. I cooked a delicious dinner and sat down to eat with my family, ready for a relaxing mealtime.

My two older children are excellent eaters. Foster, however, as I mentioned previously, likes his four food items and only those four food items. This poses a problem for him at dinnertime, as things like Goldfish crackers and candy are not typically on the menu. In the past, we would serve him his meal, the same meal everyone else was enjoying; he might, if it was a good night, eat his bread and then go to bed hungry. However, once he entered Attitude-ville and began demanding that we acknowledge that he was no longer a baby, we decided that he should be subjected to the same mealtime rules as the older two kids. Our rules are pretty easy to follow: 1) stay at the table until you've been excused, 2) use good manners, and 3) try three bites of everything on your plate.

Rule one was simple because he was strapped into his booster seat.

Rule two was simple because he had previously learned the hard way what happens when he throws or spits his food or uses potty talk at the table.

Rule three was what got him. It's what still gets him on a regular basis.

Foster sat down, ate his bread, and was then "dud" (done). We informed him that he was not, in fact, done, and that he must try his chicken and broccoli casserole. I think he thought we were kidding.

We sat down to eat dinner at 6:00 p.m.

At 7:45, Foster was still in his chair, red-faced and puffy-eyed, snot dripping off his chin, all while his food still sat in front of him. Untouched.

To make this situation even more pathetic, at this point I had already caved a little. Since it was his first night operating by "big kid" rules, I told him that he only had to try one bite of his chicken and broccoli casserole, so as to ease him into this new way of life. I kid you not when I say that the shred of broccoli he was battling with was almost microscopic.

Now before you start crying child cruelty, let me assure you that he totally and completely understood what we were asking him to do—he simply refused to do it. I'd ask him if he was ready to get down, and he'd say, "Yes." I'd tell him to eat his broccoli, and he'd scream "NOOOOOOOOOO." He would then kick his feet and slap himself in the face. I'd ask him if he wanted to join his siblings in a bubble bath, and he'd say, "Yes." I'd tell him to eat his broccoli and he'd yell, "GUCKY BROCCOLI!" and start to gag dramatically.

#MyLittleProdigy

It had been an incredibly long week. So by the time 8:00 p.m. rolled around, I didn't know whether to laugh or cry as he still sat in his high chair, refusing to eat. How could he be so stubborn?

Then the Lord reminded me how like Foster I am.

My Heavenly Father knows what I need even before I need it, and He often serves me what I might see as "gucky broccoli" because He knows what is best for me. All I can focus on is the fact that it doesn't appear to be exactly what I want, so I scream and I kick and I cry and I have my own little standoff with God.

In the same way that, as Foster's mom, I know he needs a healthy, balanced diet to thrive, my Heavenly Father knows that I need a healthy, balanced life. The "food" He serves me has included tough moments to refine me, challenges to grow me, and answers to prayer that look very different than I thought they should.

The question is this: Do I trust Him and obey, or do I dig in my heels, refusing to eat what He has dished up for me, metaphorically speaking?

The older I get and the more intimately I know the Lord, the easier it is to trust Him. I have seen His faithfulness in my life, and I have learned more and more that if He serves me spiritual broccoli, I had best eat it, lest I miss out on what He has for my life.

But just because it's gotten easier over time doesn't mean I always choose the right response. I will very probably battle between choosing His best for me and what I think I want until I meet Him face to face. To battle this is to be human.

I love what Jesus says in Matthew 6. He is addressing what it means to truly trust and know God as our Provider and Father, what it means to submit to His plans for our good. He tells his audience (and us) not to be like the hypocrites, who claim to love and trust God in the public square so that they may be seen as holy, but to love and trust God even in the private moments when it's just God and us. He tells us to be sure to mean what we pray, that we might never offer up empty words to God, claiming to trust Him but following our flesh. He follows that up with this:

> *"Do not be like them, for your Father knows what you need before you ask him. Pray then like this: 'Our Father in heaven, hallowed be your name. Your kingdom come, your will be done, on earth as it is in heaven. Give us this day our daily bread, and forgive us our debts, as we also have forgiven our debtors. And lead us not into temptation, but deliver us from evil.'"*

This prayer exposes the ultimate trusting heart. It is a prayer of submission to the Lord. When we pray this way, we confess to Him our need for HIS kingdom to come and rule in our hearts, for HIS will to be done in our lives, and for HIS daily bread (or gucky broccoli) to be our sufficiency.

Will you join me in praying this today? Not just as a token prayer, but with the purity of heart that comes only from knowing what a mess we are apart from Him. We need Him as women, as mothers, and as wives. We need him in our singleness and in our relationships and on the good days and the bad.

Spiritual broccoli may not be what we want. But if God asks us to eat it, I truly believe it's for our good.

Too bad my son didn't feel the same way. He fell asleep at the table.

Fat Girl In A Little Stall

Does anyone remember the oldie-but-goodie movie *Tommy Boy*? If you fall remotely within the chronological confines of my generation, I know your answer has to be yes, whether you admit it or not.

Tommy Boy is the epitome of who Chris Farley was as an actor (RIP, Chris...I hope you're in a VAN down by the RIVER somewhere in heaven). It's Chris at his finest (wait, is that an oxymoron?) and it. is. hilarious. It's full of some of the best movie quotes of all time, many of which I cannot share because of the slightly questionable content. However, you've gotta love:

"Brothers don't shake hands; brothers gotta hug!"

"Holy schnikes!"

"I can't hear you; you're trailing off. And did I hear a niner in there? Were you calling from a walkie-talkie?"

And of course, my favorite and yours:

"Fat guy in a little coat..."

I recently had a Chris Farley-esque incident like this. Knowing how much you enjoy laughing ~~at~~ with me when it comes to my ~~unlucky~~ charmed life, I thought I'd share how this...AHEM..."curvy" lady got stuck in the world's smallest bathroom stall. As a personal challenge, I have even taken it upon myself to use the aforementioned story as a springboard for spiritual application. We'll see how that goes.

Last year, I was invited to sing in a friend's wedding. The event was held at the historic Fabulous Fox Theatre in downtown Atlanta, and it *is* pretty fabulous. It's uber-fancy, and for a suburban mom like me (who makes it through 50% of my days without a shower or makeup), attending this lovely event at the Fox was borderline Elly May Clampett comes to town.

It was a formal wedding. At this point in my life, I am not much into cocktail-and-beyond attire, so I scrambled to find something appropriate to wear. I donned a red dress with long, flowy sleeves and even squeezed my feet into my black, sequined, peep-toed heels.

I was foxy.

I left the kids at home and prepared for a night out on the town (solo, because my hubs had a previous engagement). I was feeling free. I arrived at the wedding. I sound-checked. I sang (full disclosure: it was mediocre, at best). And then it was time for the fun part: the reception.

I visited with friends, snacked on mini-bruschetta and stuffed mushrooms, and had a nice glass of red. All was right with the world.

Dinner was served and, after a delicious meal with great company, I realized I needed to find the facilities. I excused myself and found the restroom, which was located one floor above the ballroom.

This bathroom was the jam. Seriously. I half expected an attendant to be waiting inside the toilet stall with an offer to wipe for me. Everything was fancy: fancy soaps, fancy lotions, mouthwashes, real towels with which to dry your hands, sofas and lounges (once I saw a bathroom with lounge chairs, I knew I would hold all bathrooms to that standard for the rest of my years). Basically, Elly May (that's me) had just entered potty heaven.

There were several women in the restroom ahead of me, so I had to wait for a few minutes. I was last in line, and I was super happy when I finally saw an open stall. I entered it and closed the door, of course turning the little knob in front of me to lock it in place. I relieved myself. (I always think that when one says one relieved oneself, it sounds so sophisticated; know what I mean?)

After I stood back up and got my Spanx adjusted (aww, yeah...you know it, ladies), I reached forward and turned the knob to unlock my bathroom stall. The knob turned, and I pulled on the door to open it.

Nothing.

Perplexed, I peered a little closer and realized the lock was still in place. This was weird because I had definitely turned the knob. I wiggled the knob back and forth a few more times.

Still nothing.

It was in this moment that I grew slightly concerned. Being the Sherlock that I am, I had deduced, based on the number of times I had frantically turned the knob back and forth, that the lock had somehow broken, leaving me trapped in the (very tiny) bathroom stall.

This was a very big problem, for the following reasons:

1. There wasn't a soul in sight. Somehow the ladies' room had emptied out, leaving me, by default, as the sole proprietor.
2. The way the stall was designed was not conducive to an easy escape. The space between the bottom of the stall and the floor was, to put it mildly, narrow. The stalls were also quite tall, which meant that climbing over the door was probably out of the question.
3. I was attempting to navigate this...er...situation in a formal dress and black, sequined, peep-toed heels.

I stood patiently for more than a few minutes, certain that if the number of people making rounds at the bar were any indicator, there would be an influx of twenty-somethings flooding the bathroom at any moment.

The bathroom remained empty.

After about fifteen minutes of waiting, I really did start panicking a little. I called out in a sing-song voice.

"Helloooooooooooooo?"

Nothing.

"HELLLLLLLLOOOOOOOOOOOOOOOOO?"

Nothing. That's when the yelling started.

"SOMEBODY? ANYBODY? CAN YOU HEAR ME??? HELLO?????"

Nothing.
I felt like the rapture had occurred and I was left behind. Or that I was on *The Walking Dead*, or something equally as creepy.
Finally I decided, as any foxy-and-fancy independent woman might, that I had to take the situation into my own hands.
I started out by standing on the toilet and attempting to hoist myself over the wall into the next stall. When I found myself fearing for my life, I decided against any more attempts. There is a lot of me to hoist these days, and I felt like I might end up being the photo subject of many a meme if things went poorly.
I came to the conclusion that my only option would be to squeeze my foxy self underneath the door, navigating myself through the very small space left there by the brilliant bathroom designer who obviously didn't account for women getting accidentally locked in the bathroom stall.
Now, regarding what happened next, I will paint as delicate a mental picture as I can for you, as it might otherwise lead to permanent scarring.
First, I got down on all fours, my legs straddling the toilet (point of humiliation #1). Next, I lay down flat on my stomach and approached the opening between the door and the floor as I imagine a rat might do if he

were trying to get into a cute little French bistro from a cobblestone street because he wanted a nibble of delicious cheese. Except that instead of a cobblestone street, I was lying prostrate on a pee-and-germ-covered stone-cold floor, and instead of trying to get a nibble of cheese, I found myself wishing that I hadn't eaten quite so much cheese. I knew that flattening my body one section at a time in order to work my way out was going to be challenging, to put it mildly. (The Spanx helped, of course. Let's all pause for a round of applause for their inventor, Ms. Sara Blakely.)

And so began a few moments of contorting that'd I rather not rehash. Let's just say it was something you wouldn't have been able to unsee.

The maneuvering was accompanied by groans and grunts I didn't know I could make. Actually, if I hadn't been so distracted by trying to avoid becoming a permanent fixture in the Fabulous Fox Theatre's bathroom, I probably would have been very proud of myself. I am now.

I made it to a point where I saw the proverbial light at the end of the tunnel. I was out of the stall to my rear end, and one cheek had just been freed. As I worked feverishly to slowly squish the other one into submission, what to my wondering eyes should appear but two human beings. Old human beings, to be specific.

In my most vulnerable (and impressive) moment, who should happen upon me in the until-that-moment-vacant women's restroom but two old ladies, both frozen in place and staring at me in horror.

I guess they had never seen Elly May work her way out of a bathroom stall, hillbilly style.

I stared at them. They stared at me. I started laughing and trying to explain. One said nothing. The other "tsk'ed" under her breath and made some unfunny comment like, "Well, it's a little early in the evening for you to be laid out on the bathroom floor, isn't it?"

You might think they had mercy and helped me get the remainder of myself free from the stall. You'd have thought wrong, though, because they just stood there and stared at me while I pancaked my rear end one last time and finally broke free from the stall door. They stood and stared while I stumbled to my feet in my black sequined heels and tried, ~~unsuccessfully,~~

to brush the disgusting, probably urine-covered debris off the front of my dress. They stared while I readjusted my Spanx (which had taken quite a beating) and washed my hands in scalding water. They stared as I squared my shoulders and sauntered out of the restroom, unsuccessfully attempting to play it cool.

I arrived back downstairs at my table and immediately asked why no one had come to the bathroom in almost twenty minutes. My friend explained that there had been wedding-y things going on, like special dances and blah blah blah, and so everyone was seated and attentive to the bride and groom.

Of course. Just my luck.

While everyone else was enjoying themselves, I was stuck up in a tiny stall, afraid I was never going to get out.

And isn't life like that sometimes?

I can only speak for myself, but I have to say that there are plenty of days when it seems like everyone but me is coasting through life, enjoying the ride and relaxing, while I am trapped in yet another tight spot, pressed in on every side. I know this isn't actually the case, because everyone is fighting his own battles, but it doesn't stop me from feeling that way.

Sometimes it feels like I just can't win. Like trouble follows me like a little black raincloud. Like I'm being attacked on every side. Can anyone else relate?

What I'm coming to understand more and more is that those who are in Christ have a very real enemy, an enemy who is much scarier and more evil than the bathroom-door ghost who locked me in a stall. This enemy's name is Satan, and he's out for the kill. He doesn't mess around. He loves to knock us down and then kick our legs out from under us again and again as we try to get back up. As my five-year-old son says, "He's a butt." (He's very proud that he gets to call Satan a butt, because calling anyone else that name is off-limits in our house.)

Satan wants us to live our lives feeling trapped in our circumstances and fearful of the future. He wants nothing more than for us to doubt God's sovereignty and goodness. He wants us to feel abandoned and forgotten.

He knows our weaknesses and what buttons to push, and he loves nothing more than to make us miserable. He's the commander of an entire army, and this army is constantly using new tactics to try to destroy us. They're out for our souls.

My husband puts it best when he says that the spiritual battle that's going on around us is more intense than what's happening in Afghanistan or Syria at this very moment. It's strategic and real, and we have to be mindful of it.

But—and this is a big but (not a big butt)—we know Who wins both the battle and the war. We may be knocked down, but we're not out. We might be injured, but it's not fatal. Satan can come at us with all he's got, but he doesn't have enough weapons in his arsenal to put a dent in the armor of God. Amen?

When we're in the middle of the battle and we feel like we're about to be overtaken, our only job is to remember who God says He is and to believe Him to be faithful. That's it.

Paul wrote all about his struggles and hardships in his letter to the Church of Corinth. I love what he said in 2 Corinthians 4 (this is my own compilation of several verses):

> *We are hard pressed on every side, but not crushed;*
> *perplexed, but not in despair; persecuted, but not abandoned;*
> *struck down, but not destroyed...therefore, we do not lose*
> *heart. Though outwardly we are wasting away, inwardly we*
> *are being renewed day by day. For our light and momentary*
> *troubles are achieving for us an eternal glory that far*
> *outweighs them all...*

When we feel pressed, we can know with certainty that we will not be crushed. When we are confused, we can fully know peace. When we feel beat down, we can know we are not left alone. When life hurts or when our enemy strikes us down, we can know we will get back up.

I believe that God is trustworthy and that His promises are true. He has never failed me, and I don't believe He will fail you. My prayer is that He gives us the faith we need to cling to Him in the midst of the battles of this life.

We might get knocked down, but we're never out. Let's stick it to Satan and get back up, shall we? Because after all, Satan is a butt.

PHONE CALLS FROM PRESCHOOL

"Hi, Mrs. Watts? Yes, we need you to come in and talk to your son's teacher after class. He stuck his rear end out of the bathroom and showed the whole classroom how the toilet paper stayed stuck in his bottom when he clenched his butt cheeks together."

—*A former preschool teacher*

IX

An Open Letter

"I'm not fat, I'm just short for my weight."

—Me

Dear Lady Who Just Asked Me When I'm Due:

Alas, your eyes have deceived you, for it is not a tiny human growing in my uterus, but instead a food baby growing in my gelatinous abdominal region. I can see how your eyes might have played tricks on you, though, because my food baby has grown in girth since giving birth to my actual babies (which is amazingly ironic, right?).

Let me first say: please don't feel bad.

Well, okay, it wouldn't make me totally upset if you felt a little bit bad. No, a little more bad than that. C'mon, you can feel a little worse if you put some muscle into it! Okay, that's good.

Please don't feel too bad. My FUPA (that stands for fat upper pubic area; I figured I should give you a definition because you're ~~ignorant~~ old) and I forgive you. We really do. We don't hold grudges, just calories.

We do, however, request that you do not ever, not ever, like, NEVER again assume someone is pregnant, even if they are lying in the middle of a sidewalk screaming with labor pains and covered in amniotic fluid. (Too much?) Here's a tip from The Ladies' Code of Social Correctness

Handbook: it's okay to ask someone about her pregnancy ONLY if she has first mentioned that she is, in fact, pregnant. Otherwise, just assume it's a mommy muffin.

Capisce?

I have given birth to three children. My fourth is stubbornly refusing to leave my body, and I am well aware of this. Don't get me wrong; I'm no Mama June, but I do have a slight case of dunlop disease. (You know, when one's belly done lops over one's pants?) My upper arms now sport a nice pair of bingo wings.

All I can say is that I'm working on it. And I'm okay.

The "I'm okay" part is a big deal, because, you see, there was a period of time in my life (most of my life, really) when I wouldn't have been okay. I used to fight an eating disorder. I was thin. I was svelte. I was fit. I was horribly proud. And I was miserable.

Then I got freed up by the Lord and, quickly thereafter, had three kids. My body was not my own (and apparently still isn't). I was left with stretch marks galore, lumps where I shouldn't have lumps, and cellulite on my kneecaps. My muscle tone diminished. I grew tired and overrun and didn't have time to spend in the gym like I once did. And yes, I know you might have been the mom who stayed fit all through pregnancy and dropped the weight like a champ, but have some grace for the rest of us, please and thank you.

I'm kind of a mess, physically. And I'm working on it.

And it's okay.

You see, I have come to realize that I traded something temporary, my "perfect" body and my fitness bragging rights, for something eternal. Three children. Three souls. Three tiny humans that I hope and pray will one day grow into mighty warriors for the kingdom of God. Three lives that I have the privilege and responsibility to shape and mold.

So do I shape and mold myself, my own body? In other words, do I care for myself physically and pursue health?

Yes.

However.

What I pursue even more, and what I see as the best trade-off I'll ever have made, is growing my children up as best I can into honorable, noble, godly adults who live lives of integrity and purpose. And if I have a food baby for the rest of my life because I can't commit as many hours to the gym as I'd like (and because, let's be honest, mothers have no abs), so be it.

> *Behold, children are a heritage from the Lord, the fruit of the womb a reward. Like arrows in the hand of a warrior are the children of one's youth.*

PSALM 127:3–4

I am making a conscious effort to focus on things that matter. Things with eternal value.

If my food baby does decide, however, that it's time to let go of her death grip around my middle section and succumb to the powers of arugula and the elliptical machine, I wouldn't be mad. Wait…that probably means that I should get on an elliptical machine and eat arugula occasionally, doesn't it? I think I'm starting to get it!

STUFF I NEVER THOUGHT I'D SAY

*"Do NOT sling your pee all over the lawnmower,
especially when it's parked in the garage!"*

—*Me, to my proud three-year-old son*

X

Aha!

"By Jove, I think she's got it!"

—Prof. Henry Higgins (*My Fair Lady*)

This chapter wasn't in the original outline I wrote for this book. In fact, the event that propelled my desired to write this chapter didn't even take place until this morning as I was preparing to disembark (or is it debark? Or disboard? Get off? You get the idea though, right?) the cruise ship on which I spent the last five days. However, in light of the previous chapter, my open letter both to foot-in-mouth-type people everywhere and for women who struggle with body image insecurities, I knew immediately that I had to write about it.

As I have mentioned, I went on a cruise by myself for two reasons: 1) to write this book, and 2) to get some R & R. Both goals were accomplished and hopefully accomplished well. I enjoyed my time alone. I found that I am great company for myself. I am very fun to be with.

However, last night, as I sat in the karaoke lounge and listened to a very enthusiastic, inebriated singer belt out her best version of Whitney Houston's "I Wanna Dance With Somebody," I found myself a little down and dejected. I felt insecure. And you're gonna laugh when you hear why (it's okay; I'm kind of laughing, too, partly out of shame and partly because it's totally ridiculous).

I had been sitting with me, myself, and I for a while when a lady asked if she could join me. I obliged, of course, and she sat down on the other end of the sofa. She reeked of cigarettes and looked like the majority of her days had been spent in a tanning bed that was cranked up to eleven. I honestly didn't know if her age was fifty or seventy-five, but she was nice enough. Upon sitting down, she immediately started asking me probing questions.

"Where are you from? Who did you come on this cruise with? What do you mean, you came alone? You mean, like, *alone*-alone? Are you married? Why didn't your husband come? Did you not want him to come?"

And on and on and on. Then, "How many guys did you pick up?"

I almost choked on my water when she asked me that. I started laughing hysterically, then answered with an emphatic, "NONE!"

She stared at me like I had three heads. "None? Are you serious?"

I assured her that I was, in fact, dead serious, and that my husband probably wouldn't have liked it if I "picked up" guys on my solo cruise.

"Well, aren't you a nice girl," she said, semi-sarcastically. "I couldn't get the men on this ship to leave me alone. I'll admit, I did hook up with a few of them, but it's okay—what happens on Carnival stays on Carnival, am I right? Just don't tell my husband!"

I stared at her, at a loss for words. And then…wait for it…I started feeling…I can't even believe I'm going to tell you this…*jealous*.

Yes, you read that correctly.

I. Was. Jealous. It disgusts me even as I type the words.

It wasn't that I wished I had taken the opportunity to hook up with a few dudes on the ship, because I'd never in a million years betray my husband, even if I somehow had the desire to do so. My man more than satisfies me.

I was jealous because she, this crazy smoker tan lady, had been noticed. And I hadn't.

I hadn't considered the fact that men hadn't taken advantage of my singleness and flocked to hit on me until this lady pointed it out. And I honestly didn't want any man, creepy or totally legit, to hit on me. Until this lady showed up.

Then, I sorta-kinda wished someone had tried to at least chat me up, so I would have felt noticed. This is so embarrassing to admit.

#MyCheeksAreRed

I went back to my stateroom and stared at my naked self in the mirror (bad idea). Everything I wrote in the previous chapter about being at peace with my body and being focused on the things that really matter in life went out the window and into the Gulf of Mexico. I was not okay. I was disgusted with myself. I was angry with myself. How could I have let myself get to the point where men don't hit on me?

I journaled and prayed and fell into restless sleep. I knew the truth God was speaking to me, but I didn't like it. I didn't want to receive it. I wanted to be hit-on-able!

This morning, I packed my suitcase, gathered my things, and went to the elevators near my room to hitch a ride upstairs to the breakfast buffet so I could grab a cuppa before I deplaned. I mean deported. Huh?

As the elevator doors opened, I stepped into the car and joined two men who were already headed up, both of whom turned out to be captains of the ship, and both of whom were very handsome. I smiled and said good morning.

One of them looked at me, then turned to the other man and said, "This is the woman I was telling you about, the one I saw last night by the pool."

I jerked my face up and stared at him, then I gracefully said something like, "Huh?"

He said, "I watched you last night for a long time as you sat and talked to the bartender. You talked to her and asked about her life. You smiled with your eyes and you were kind. When I finished my break, I went back to work and told him (pointing at the other captain dude) that I had just observed the happiest lady I think I have ever seen. You were a pleasure to watch."

I think my jaw was on the ground. At the very same time, my heart was breaking. Then it was ashamed. Then it understood. Then it was redeemed.

"I...uh...am generally pretty happy," I stuttered, at a loss for anything else to say. We reached my floor; then the elevator door opened, and I walked out into the atrium. As I turned around and waved, the captain said with a smile, "Keep spreading happy, okay?"

That elevator ride was a game-changer for me. By Jove, I GET IT! And I hope and pray I never, ever forget it. Don't let me forget it, okay?

See, I chose to pity myself the night before, focusing on my lumps and my abundance of curves and the lies that the enemy was spoon-feeding me. All of my insecurities came out to play, and although I wasn't looking to receive a man's attention while I was away by myself, I somehow felt shafted that I hadn't gotten it. This was all rooted in my flesh and my insecurities, and it revealed the nastiest, most sin-filled parts of me.

God chose to remind me what really matters, and He did so through a cruise ship captain and a chance encounter with a sweet bartender from the Philippines. She made me a rockin' margarita and told me about her life and about her struggles as a single mom. About her son who is living with her mother in Manila while she, his mom, spends ten months a year working seven days a week, twelve hours a day on a cruise ship in order to send him to private school and, hopefully, on to college. I listened. I prayed. And I tried to encourage her and remind her that God loves her and that she is not forgotten.

And that moment was the moment I captured a man's attention. And he noticed me for my inner beauty.

Thank you, Jesus, for Your beauty in me, even when my ugliness threatens to overshadow it. Thank You for allowing me to wallow in my self-pity and insecurity just long enough to see the stark contrast between physical beauty and inner radiance.

You don't know how badly I want to "keep spreading happy."

And y'all, I've got to throw this in as well, just because it proves that God has a fantastic sense of humor. After I made my way off the ship and through customs, I boarded a shuttle bus to take me back to the Miami Airport and sat down in the first available seat. Across the aisle from me, I heard a loud, raspy voice holler out, "A pretty thing like you, traveling all alone?"

I looked sideways and found a ninety-ish-year-old man staring at me through his Coke-bottle glasses.

"I wish I'd have laid eyes on you the day we set sail. You and me, we coulda spent some time together!"

I don't think I have ever laughed so hard in my entire life.

As we got off the bus and headed into the airport, he yelled, "Honey, this cruise ain't over 'til I hit the ground in Philly. Wanna have some fun?"

Well played, God. Well played.

<u>STUFF MY FRIENDS' KIDS SAY</u>

*"Mommy, how come you have all THIS
if there's no baby in there?"*

—*My friend's daughter, as she squeezed
the flesh on her mom's stomach*

XI

Words

"Be sure to taste your words before you spit them out."

—Unknown

My son asked me last week if God "tooters" up in heaven. When I answered that, no, I don't guess He does, because God doesn't have a body like a man so he probably doesn't have methane building up inside His non-existent intestines.

Sutton then asked me if people "tooter" up in heaven. I could have told him that they don't right now, but once their physical bodies are resurrected after Christ returns to earth they might just stink up the halls of heaven.

But I didn't. I didn't think he was ready for that theology yet.

Kids say the darndest things, don't they? I never lack for something to laugh about when I listen to my kids talk. Except for that time when Foster went through the terrible threes.

It's hard to be three and a half years old.

No, it's not. When you're three and a half, life's a breeze. When you're three and a half and the youngest of three children, life is a DOUBLE-breeze. Everybody does everything for you. All you have to do is point, and whoever's around plays real-life search-and-find, rummaging through the cupboard shelves, trying to locate the delicious snack item on which you have your mind set. Goldfish? No. Cheeze-Its? Double-no. Granola bar? FOOT-STOMPING NO! All of this while you don't use your words. Because you don't have to use your words. Because you're three and a half and the youngest of three children and somehow, at some time, people decided they just don't care anymore about teaching you to be a civilized human being.

The time had come for my littlest buckaroo to use his words. Pronto.

The phrase "the terrible twos" is very deceptive. The twos have troubling moments, to be sure, but that year is a cakewalk compared to the threes. The twos are "terrible lite." If you have a two-year-old and you're thinking, "Surely she doesn't know what she's talking about, because the twos have been the pits in my house," I advise you now to sit down. Pour yourself a cold one. And prepare yourself for the truth bomb that's about to be dropped on you.

Ready?

The threes are worse. Everyone who has a child that is three years or older is nodding her head right now, silently pitying you because she intimately knows the storm that's headed your way. There is no escaping the tortuous threes. I'm sorry.

When your little cherub turns three, you, too, might be dealing with scenarios such as those I'm about to describe. Don't look away; I know you'll want to, but don't do it. Consider it my gift to you, some preparation for what's to come (because it doesn't just happen to me, right? RIGHT?).

SCENARIO 1:
A note from his preschool teacher:

"Jordan, Foster had a very hard day today. He hit Ana in the face and he keeps following boys into the bathroom, waiting for them to pull down their pants to pee and then pinching their butts. He was on the red behavior chart today [obviously]."

SCENARIO 2:
A note from his preschool teacher:

"Jordan, Foster did not have a good day at all. It started well, but then he told me that he was going to 'kick me in the face,' and things went downhill after that. He was on red today [again, obviously]."

SCENARIO 3:
A phone call from his preschool teacher:

"Jordan? It's Shannon. Listen, Foster just bit Connor because he wanted the toy Connor was playing with. Normally, he would get sent home for this, but I'm going to give him a little grace [probably because he's cute]. Needless to say, he's gonna be on red today."

This is just a small sampling of my precious son's behavior at age three. It happened at home, too, but the events at school were more embarrassing. I know it sounds like he's undisciplined and probably gets away with murder, but, all joking aside, we have always been on that kid like white on rice. We are consistent. We are loving. We teach him the truths of God's Word and we don't put up with hitting or biting or pinching or telling people they are going to get a swift kick in the face.

And still he persevered. I have to give it to him—he sticks to his guns! I am praying it serves him and the world well one day, because in his early childhood it typically ends up just resulting in the raining down of consequence upon consequence.

His problem was that, especially because he's the baby, he was under the impression that he doesn't have to use his words. Someone took his crayon? He hit them. Someone had a toy he wanted? He bit them to get it. Someone went pee? He pinched them. (Okay, I can't explain that one away...it's just weird.)

In the Watts house, we get creative with discipline. I learned from the master herself, my mother. My hubby is also creative, and sometimes it's very hard not to laugh while we throw down the fiery wrath of discipline upon our kids.

In order to explain, let me give you an example of the way we discipline in relation to the three scenarios I painted for you a moment ago.

SCENARIO 1: Foster hit (a girl) and pinched (boys' butts).

In this case, Foster earned himself the privilege of wearing wool mittens for an entire day. In the 80-degree weather. Because, quite simply, if he cannot use his hands for kindness, then he will wear gloves on his hands to remind him that his choices have consequences, and that he should use his words and not his hands if someone takes his crayon. He was given the "opportunity" to wear these gloves to preschool and was told he could not take them off unless he was eating or going potty. His hands got sweaty. He had trouble holding his crayons. He was clumsy with toys. It was perfect.

SCENARIO 2: Foster told his teacher he was going to kick her in the face.

Wow, even typing that description is horrifying. I promise you, he's not "that kid." You know, the one society needs to fear? I have no doubt he's going to be something great, because God sure did give him guts! He's not afraid of much, including saying things for sheer shock value. In our home, we don't call names and we SURE don't threaten bodily harm to adults (or anyone, for that matter). We have a little bottle of what we affectionately refer to as "sassy sauce" for situations such as this (it's apple cider vinegar). He received a healthy dose. I think I can still smell it on his breath, too.

SCENARIO 3: Foster bit Connor (sorry, Connor's mom).

I'm sure you understand how it feels to have your child bite the new kid in class. Anyone? No one? Here's how it feels in one word: horrifying. It feels horrifying. Biting is a big deal, and my other kids didn't really deal with habitual biting. They did it once or twice, and that was that. Not Foster. Like I said, he sticks with it. We tried (almost) everything, and even then I got that dreaded phone call from school. Count Dracula strikes again!

I was steaming mad, I won't lie. After weeks of dealing with his stupid choices and bad behavior, I was tired. of. it. With my mom's help and great advice, I decided to take extreme measures. Thank goodness we have a random supply of surgical masks for situations such as this (or Ebola, of course).

How do you communicate to an almost-four-year-old child that he has to learn to use his words to solve problems instead of using his body? How do you teach him that words count, even things said as a joke or simply for shock value? Yes, I know, he wasn't even four yet. But he was smart, and he knew better.

How could I teach him to use his words when I misuse my own words—and often?

It starts with me and with you, moms and dads. Like it or not, it starts with us. Before we can throw Proverbs out to our kids, before we can come down on them for not handling conflict well and with love and gentleness, we have to practice it ourselves. We have to learn to use our words in a healthy way.

Proverbs is full of wisdom on the subject of using our words for good:

The words of the reckless pierce like swords, but the tongue of the wise brings healing.

PROVERBS 12:18

Kind words are like honey—sweet to the soul and healthy for the body.

Proverbs 16:24

When words are many, transgression is not lacking, but whoever restrains his lips is prudent.

PROVERBS 10:19

Death and life are in the power of the tongue, and those who love it will eat its fruits.

PROVERBS 18:21

And of course, one of my favorite Psalms:

Let the words of my mouth and the meditation of my heart be acceptable in your sight, O Lord, my rock and my redeemer.

PSALM 19:14

Sometimes I need a dose of sassy sauce. I don't pinch or bite or punch anymore, but my words often do just as much damage—maybe even more. We have to lead the way for our kids, and I obviously need to do a better job!

So how do we do this, practically speaking? How do we turn an idea into action? I think that, most importantly, we have to engage regularly with the Lord, bringing to Him an attitude of honesty and humility. How can we expect ourselves to have a filter on our mouths if we haven't guarded ourselves with a filter on our hearts? When we fill ourselves up with the Presence and Word of God, He is what comes out when our mouths open. Our hearts must be yielded to Him, and we must be constantly striving to honor him with our lives, including our words. He promises to give us everything we need for life and godliness, and He will be faithful to that end. But we have to make ourselves available, and we have to empty ourselves of everything that is not of Him.

#TheHardestWork

I pray that the words of my mouth—and yours—will be acceptable in the sight of the Lord, and that our words will be a sweet and healing balm for all who hear them.

Also, boys are dumb.

<u>STUFF MY KIDS SAY</u>

When asked what she had dreamt about the previous night:
"I dreamed about Jesus. And my long, beautiful hair."

—Emerson Watts, age 3

XII

Perseverance

*"Survival can be summed up in three words: never give up.
That's the heart of it, really. Just keep trying."*

—Bear Grylls

The Grocery Store Curse

I believe the Word of God is infallible. It's inspired. It's a literary masterpiece. However, in the beginning of the book of Genesis, shortly after Adam and Eve seriously jacked up our futures by eating that forbidden fruit, I am pretty sure God left out a section that read something like this:

> To the woman he said, *"I will surely multiply your pain in childbearing; in pain you shall bring forth children."*
>
> [ADDITION: *"And you shall forever be subject to taking said children grocery shopping with you, and it shall be a terrible plight each and every time. Also, you shall never again pee alone."*]

(GENESIS 3:16A—PLUS THE PART I JUST MADE UP)

Forgive me if I sound flippant with Scripture, but anyone who has been a mom for more than five minutes knows what I am talking about. Every mom has silently ~~cussed~~ thanked Eve under her breath more than once while strolling the aisles of Publix with a long grocery list and a child who suddenly feels the need to engage in a deep-meaning-of-life-type question-and-answer session, intermixed with loud, "Can we get thats?!?!"

I am being very serious when I say that nothing reminds me of my need for Jesus' help in parenting more than a family trip to the grocery store. It really does seem like the worst comes out in everyone, parents and children alike, during this seemingly never-ending task.

I often feel set up to fail before I even step foot inside the store. Oh, everyone is happy and cooperative on the car ride there. The first sign of distress typically occurs as we exit our awesome blue minivan and I ask my children to hold hands so we can play Frogger through the parking lot. At some point between the van and the sidewalk, one or more of my children decide that they are too big to hold hands. At this point, they determine that the best solution to their problem is to go limp like a cooked noodle, making it impossible for anyone to hold their hand lest they, too, fall to the asphalt. This is usually where "consequence" number one is tallied and tucked away for later, when we get home.

Once we get everyone into the grocery store, my children make a bee-line to the race car. You know the one: the double-seater that has pretend steering wheels and more germs than a toilet seat at the airport. Enter dilemma number two: which two of my three children will have the distinct pleasure of sitting in the buggy, and which one will walk? An argument typically ensues based upon who does or does not want to ride that day, who got to ride "last time," and who is a "big kid" that doesn't need to ride in a cart anymore.

Once I get everyone ~~duct-taped~~ strapped in, I tentatively enter the store through the automatic sliding doors. Our favorite check-out lady, Tina, sees me and starts laughing immediately, probably sensing the chaos that is getting ready to ensue as the Watts family takes over Publix.

First stop: the bakery, of course. Oh, the joy that a free, dried-out sugar cookie can elicit in the heart of a child. Every mother knows that you must have a grocery list either mentally or physically prepared upon arriving at the bakery, because the moment those cookies enter the hands of your children, an imaginary timer starts ticking away the portion of your shopping experience that can be done in silence and peace. The younger the kid is, the longer the cookie lasts, thus yielding a calmer, more orderly grocery run. The older the kid is, the faster he eats and the faster Mom goes from "I can actually hear myself think" to the overwhelming temptation to "ABORT MISSION!"

With cookies in hand, the shopping begins, and for a few moments everything is as it should be. Then, inevitably, the child who is supposed to be trailing behind me but instead ends up in front of the cart to "help" by pulling it down the aisle then stops suddenly, causing me to ram the cart right into her Achilles tendon.

Cue the waterworks. I begin to apologize repeatedly while my daughter gives me the death stare for hurting her, even though she was the one who walked in front of the cart to begin with. She limps her way behind the cart and climbs in, switching places with my middle son, because her leg hurts. It is now his turn to walk with me.

We make a stop at the deli counter, where I order two sub sandwiches that take fifteen (yes, that's FIFTEEN) minutes to prepare. I almost think I should double check to see if they are custom slaughtering the animals out back for the daily special.

Their cookies long since devoured, the kids are already asking when we're leaving and when they can have a snack. My daughter doesn't want my youngest touching "her" steering wheel and, of course, all my son wants to do is touch "her" steering wheel, so things are at a bit of an impasse. Suffice it to say the race car seat is not a happy place.

While this is transpiring, my middle son is smearing his hands along the glass deli case, leaving trails of cookie grease and who-knows-what-else. The sandwich-maker man looks rather perturbed that I have children that are behaving like…children, which one might think would make him work faster—but no. The line is growing behind me as a hungry crowd of lunchgoers wait their turns to buy a mediocre, overpriced sandwich.

Just as Mr. Sandwich Man is finally handing me my subs, my son comes up behind me and lifts my sundress with both hands, exposing my bare, pasty-white rear end that is semi-covered with ratty, torn navy blue thong underwear, along with a baseball-sized black bruise on my left butt cheek from the antibiotic shot I received days before to treat me for strep throat (that my kids gave me). I hear laughter filter through the crowd of people with a rear view (at least ten people were in line for sandwiches behind us).

At this point in my life, however, someone seeing my hind end is the least of my concerns. Truthfully, it's worse for them because witnessing my backside in all its glory is something they will never be able to unsee. I continue my delightful journey, fairly unfazed.

As we move along, we arrive at the juice aisle, the aisle created by some kind of parent-hating genius. Not only are there multicolored bottles of fun-looking drinks and juice boxes packaged in Pixar-character print, but there are swirly straws and reusable drink containers hanging every five feet, right at eye level with my children. The "Mommy, can we's" start before I can even turn that fateful corner.

"Oh, Mommy, puh-leeeeeaaaase can I get a new Princess cup? I never had one like that before!"

"Mom, look, a Doth Fadah cup with a light-savah straw! Please, please, please, please can I get it?"

Even the baby gets in on the action, grunting, "Uhhhhh" while pointing at cheaply made, dishwasher-unsafe cups that wouldn't last a day in my house.

After a long string of "no, no, nos" and "don't ask me agains," on we go.

At this point, I feel the need to step up my game in order to get this job over and done with. So our walk becomes brisker and my patience runs admittedly thinner...as does my children's. They go from wanting fun kid stuff to just wanting everything they see for the sake of buying something, anything, to meet their western-world-shopping-addiction needs. Pretty soon, they are wanting GladWare and toilet paper and maybe a bottle of olive oil.

Right about now, my son reaches his hand out of the cart in time to make contact with a large display of paper towels, bringing down the pyramid with a single touch. Can anyone page for a cleanup on aisle ten? While frantically trying to gather the millions of rolls of paper towels, my daughter decides that she wants to "help" me by pushing the cart out of the way. Push, she does, right into the large wooden crate of wine bottles. I'll let you guess what happens from there.

#IWishIWereLying

I finally look up from our disaster zone to find a multitude of people staring at me. Some have pity in their eyes, while others are looking at me with disgust. And, of course, there's the one old lady who feels the need to tell me in this moment to "enjoy every single minute with those precious little ones."

To which I offer her a "cheers" as I start chugging from the broken, half-empty bottle of wine on the floor because it's no use crying over spilled wine.

I know that I just have to push through to the end of our excursion, which is in sight. No matter if everyone is crying, no matter if my children are annihilating each other, no matter if people look at me like I am the worst mother in the history of mothers, my people gotta eat, so we go on. I stop for no man. Or child. My children see in my eyes that I am not to be toyed with, and they are brought to (momentary) silence.

We grab the last of our produce and whip back around toward the registers. Amazingly, with nineteen registers lining the front of the store, two are open. One is for hoarders like me; the other is for the twenty-items-or-less people who shop more than once every ten days. And even though her line is empty, I can see it in her eyes: the twenty-items-or-less lady ain't gonna budge and let me through because I am over the limit. Her head shakes slightly. I sigh and get in the four-person-long line at the other register.

As we finally approach the cashier, the begging for candy and gum begins.

"Mom, you NEVER let us get gum. Puh-leeeaseeee?"

"Mom, please can I have M&M's? But, Mom, I asked POLITELY!"

It's about this time that I tune out and go to my happy place.

We get to the register to find that the man checking us out is very friendly and talkative. He is also extremely effeminate, both in his mannerisms and in the way he sounds. So just to make a fun morning that much better, my inquisitive middle son feels the need to ask him: "Hey, man, why do you talk like such a girl?"

#PalmToFace

At this point, I'm exhausted, so I can't even pretend that it didn't happen. I just mutter a "sorry" and wait on him to finish ringing me up. I don't even flinch at the total, because the emotional toll this trip has taken on me is far more painful than the current cost of groceries. I swipe my AmEx so that I can be done with this experience for good.

As I put my credit card away, my four-year-old presses the red "cancel" button. I, in my calmest and most calculated tone, ask him not to touch the machine again. I take my credit card out once more, swiping it while doling out another consequence-once-we-get-home to my daughter, who has just swatted her youngest brother.

Again, as I put my card away, my middle rascal presses the cancel button.

Seriously? The cashier doesn't even attempt to hide his grin, somewhat deservedly. The 80-something lady in line behind me, the one who resembles Joan Rivers (if you live in Atlanta, you know what I am talking about; there are old-lady Joan Rivers lookalikes all over town) looks disapprovingly at me, tsk-ing under her breath, probably something about "kids these days." My son is awarded consequence #2 and, after receiving "the mom look" from me, doesn't dare move while I run my card for a third time, finally paying for the food that has probably gone bad by now.

In a display of confidence-bordering-on-embarrassment, I pick up my son, grab the cart, and head out of the store, unable to look behind me for fear of the round of applause that has probably erupted upon our leaving.

We get to the van, get everyone unloaded and into their rightful car seats, and I load the groceries haphazardly into the trunk, because at this point what are a dozen broken eggs after my spirit has been crushed? Okay, that might be a little dramatic...eggs are $2/dozen now, so even with a crushed spirit, I take special care of my eggs, letting them ride in the front seat. I return the cart to the cart corral, which is always, I repeat, ALWAYS as far from my car as it can possibly be. I climb in the car to a symphony of tears, "I'm hots," and "Can we go to Chick-fil-As?"

I sit. I breathe. I am still.

This might sound a bit dramatic, but I assure you that every single thing I've written about has actually happened to me. Every. Single. Thing.

This also might sound like I have hellions for children. I do not. They are CHILDREN, and it takes one to know one, right? All of us act out at times; kids just have a knack for all acting out at the same time. They are darling, precious, loving, and kind children. But, as we've established before, they are also little sinners.

Lastly, this might sound like I am a depressed soul who caves under the pressure of motherhood. This could not be further from the truth (thank you, Lord, and thank you, Prozac). However, I feel the need to encourage other mothers that they are not, as they might think, crazy; that yes, these things do happen in other families and to other moms, and that no, they are not alone.

Not every moment of motherhood is fun. The pressure—to be supermom, to have perfectly behaved, perfectly mannered children and to soak in every precious moment of motherhood—is enormous.

But that is not reality. It's merely a façade. And when we play the game of appearing perfect for the approval of others, we become fatigued, overwhelmed, and discouraged.

Full disclosure: I am a mom who lives most days in the trenches.

You are, too.

Maybe today you just need to be reminded that you're not alone. You're really not. Motherhood is full of ups and downs, and the stark reality is that our job is to raise up little sinners to know Jesus, to love Jesus, and to love the world for the sake of Jesus.

Jesus and sin are like oil and water: they just don't mix. Because of this tension, it will always, ALWAYS be hard to avoid life in the trenches. In fact, we are guaranteed trials until the day we meet Jesus face to face and He perfects us. Until then, He reminds us:

> *In this world you will have trouble.*
> *But take heart! I have overcome the world.*

> (JOHN 16:33)

Motherhood is not easy; it's not ever going to be. But it is refining. I mean, what is more refining than having to respond with grace when your son lifts up your sundress for the world to see your cellulite-covered behind?

Motherhood is a calling; it is, perhaps, the most noble calling. We have to remember the big picture. We are trying to raise up tiny humans into grown, responsible adults that love and pursue Jesus. This takes time. This takes mistakes. This takes energy. It takes perseverance. It takes dying to ourselves day in and day out, submitting and resubmitting our will to our Heavenly Father. It takes losing what we think we need in order to gain what He KNOWS we need.

I love how Philippians 3:8–15 (ESV) describes it:

> *Indeed, I count everything as loss because of the surpassing*
> *worth of knowing Christ Jesus my Lord. For his sake I have*
> *suffered the loss of all things and count them as rubbish,*
> *in order that I may gain Christ and be found in him, not*
> *having a righteousness of my own that comes from the law,*
> *but that which comes through faith in Christ, the righteousness*
> *from God that depends on faith—that I may know him*
> *and the power of his resurrection, and may share his sufferings,*
> *becoming like him in his death, that by any means possible I*

*may attain the resurrection from the dead. Not that I have
already obtained this or am already perfect, but I press on
to make it my own, because Christ Jesus has made me his
own. Brothers, I do not consider that I have made it my own.
But one thing I do: forgetting what lies behind and straining
forward to what lies ahead, I press on toward the goal for the
prize of the upward call of God in Christ Jesus. Let those of us
who are mature think this way, and if in anything you think
otherwise, God will reveal that also to you.*

I pray that through the grocery store experiences in our lives, we will persevere and press on toward the goal and for the prize, which is the call of God in Christ. I pray that we truly do count everything as loss, including our agendas, our desire for perfection, and our pride, in order that we may gain Christ and be found in Him. I pray that we don't miss the opportunities for refinement that He extends to us and that we will not be blinded by our frustration and self-entitlement. I pray that we see Him in every single tedious, monotonous, exhausting moment that threatens to overtake us. Because He is there. And He is working.

I pray most of all that no matter how hard things get, we never give up. Life is hard. Motherhood is hard. But anything worth doing requires hard work, or so I've heard. Persevere, my friends. The prize is going to be worth it!

Lastly, I would be remiss to wrap up without offering a self-proclaimed genius idea from this everyday mom of three to my friends at Publix and all of the other grocery stores around the world. This idea is yours for the taking, and you're welcome. If you could, please and thank you, make your kiddy carts more like kiddy cages, I believe it would be to both your benefit and mine.

***P. S. If the mention of Prozac in a joking manner offends you, can I just ask you, from a heart full of the love and grace of Jesus, to relax? I am not making fun of mental illness; I actually suffer from it. Life is hard. Prozac helps. I'm thankful for smart people who do scientific stuff to discover treatments for illnesses like depression, and I'm thankful that I can laugh about it. I hope you will laugh with me!

Move Over, Billy!

I am a lot of things. And before you start calling me names, just know that I've been called worse, okay?

Seriously, though, we all wear a lot of hats. I am wife, friend, mother, singer, writer, plant-killer, baller. And, as a mom, I am a MINISTER. We all are.

Do you ever think of yourself as a minister? Or is that, in your mind, a title reserved for those who hold seminary and divinity degrees or who work on the staff of your local church? It seems that in current church culture, one can't be called a minister without specific educational or vocational credentials.

I think that most of us, when we think of a minister, visualize someone like the amazing Billy Graham. That's not a bad thing; after all, he IS pretty great—I mean, he's Billy Graham! But how often do we think of ministers as moms who've just finished a fifteen-hour workday and look like they've been through Hurricane Katrina on stun; moms covered in spit-up and poop and goodness knows what else, moms who are sleepwalking through the routine of packing school lunches and attempting to pay some bills and respond to a few emails?

That's me (and probably you, too). I have no official credentials. I haven't taken seminary courses on the twelve tribes of Israel or the genealogy of Jesus. I haven't received a certificate of ordination. But then again, neither had Paul.

One of my favorite sections of Scripture depicts just what it means to have authentic ministry, to be a true minister of the Lord. Paul and Timothy wrote about it in their letter to the church at Corinth:

> *We live in such a way that no one will stumble because of us,*
> *and no one will find fault with our ministry. In everything*

we do, we show that we are true ministers of God. We patiently endure troubles and hardships and calamities of every kind. We have been beaten, been put in prison, faced angry mobs, worked to exhaustion, endured sleepless nights, and gone without food. We prove ourselves by our purity, our understanding, our patience, our kindness, by the Holy Spirit within us, and by our sincere love. We faithfully preach the truth. God's power is working in us. We use the weapons of righteousness in the right hand for attack and the left hand for defense. We serve God whether people honor us or despise us, whether they slander us or praise us. We are honest, but they call us impostors. We are ignored, even though we are well known. We live close to death, but we are still alive. We have been beaten, but we have not been killed. Our hearts ache, but we always have joy. We are poor, but we give spiritual riches to others. We own nothing, and yet we have everything.

2 CORINTHIANS 6:3–10 (NLT)

This is a beautiful example of what it looks like to be a minister of the gospel! Our lives should mirror the ministry of Jesus Christ—we should be living lives that don't cause others to stumble, and we should be striving to have a reputation with which none can find fault. Neither Paul nor Timothy had Doctor of Divinity degrees plastered on their office walls. They didn't even have offices! Their very LIVES were their ministry.

Moms, our lives are our mission fields! Our daily grinds are where God wants us to "go and make disciples!" Here's a glimpse into what a morning on my mission field looks like:

6:25 a.m.: I wake up to my five-year-old poking me in the face with his finger, asking me to get up and get him some juice. Let me explain the rage that fills my heart when someone wakes me up by poking me in the face. It's a raging rage. A raging, rage-ful, rage-enous rage.

6:30 a.m.: I stumble to the kitchen to prepare juice for the kids, only to find that we are all out of juice, very probably because I haven't been to the grocery store in nine days. Cue the weeping and moaning over the lack of juice and the outrage over being served WATER. (This is what we refer to in my home as a first-world problem.)

6:40 a.m.: I sweep the kitchen floor.

6:55 a.m.: I prepare breakfasts and, while the kids eat, unload and reload the dishwasher.

7:05 a.m.: I sweep the kitchen floor because the breakfast crumbs are spread far and wide.

7:10 a.m.: I start the first of nine loads of laundry. Yes, nine. I have been putting it off for a couple of days. Now I'm regretting that decision.

7:15 a.m.: I sweep the kitchen floor because the boys rolled in leaves yesterday and left every bit of their crushed-up-dried-leaf goodness all over their t-shirts, which results in fresh mulch falling like confetti through the house as I sort clothes to be washed.

7:20 a.m.: Time to drive my oldest to school.

8:45 a.m.: I try to get my younger kids to go play outside in the 40-degree weather because "it'll be fun!" Translation: "Please go outside and play so I can hear myself think for five minutes." This begins the process of kids running in and out and in and out and in and out and leaving the back door wide open. Every. Single. Time.

9:30 a.m.: I sweep dirt from outside off the kitchen floor.

10:35 a.m.: My children declare themselves "STARVING" and in need of a snack. Reminder: I haven't been to the grocery store in nine days. I come up with some stale graham crackers and peanut butter, so I make cookie sandwiches. They inhale most of them, and the rest fall as crumbs to...you guessed it...the kitchen floor!

10:40 a.m.: I sweep the kitchen floor.

10:45 a.m.: I change the laundry over from the washer to the dryer.

11:30 a.m.: The kids are ready for lunch (you'd think they look like Jabba the Hutt the way they eat, but they don't). I make frozen chicken nuggets and tater tots. They eat the nuggets and then say they don't like tater tots. Who in the world DOESN'T LIKE TOTS?

12:00 p.m.: I sweep lunch leftovers off the kitchen floor.

Et cetera, et cetera, et cetera.

The life of a minister is hard. It's busy. There's always someone begging for your time and attention and help. It can be exhausting.

It can also be the most rewarding thing we will ever do, if we allow it to be.

I believe that there is great encouragement for mothers found in the examples of Paul and Timothy. In times of trial, they persevered. They chose to love in the face of disrespect. They chose patience in times of frustration. Their work was often overlooked in spite of its great importance. Sound familiar?

If you will allow me some creative license, I would love to share 2 Corinthians 6:3–10 with you again; this time, in my own words as rewritten for mothers:

We, as mothers, live in such a way that our children will not stumble because of us, and they will not find fault with our ministry. In everything we do, we show that we are true ministers of God. We patiently endure troubles and hardships and calamities of every kind. We have been whined at and spit up on; we've faced angry mobs of hungry children, worked to exhaustion, endured sleepless nights, and gone without *hot* food. We prove ourselves by our purity, our understanding, our patience, our kindness, by the Holy Spirit within us, and by our sincere love. We faithfully preach the truth to our children. God's power is working in us. We use the weapons of righteousness in the right hand for attack and the left hand for defense. We serve God whether our children honor us or despise us, whether they slander us or praise us. We are loving, but they call us mean. We are ignored, even though we are well known. We live selflessly, giving ourselves away, but we are still whole. We have been beaten down, but we have not been devoured. Our hearts ache, but we always have joy. We go without so that we might give spiritual riches to our children. We own nothing, and yet we have everything.

2 CORINTHIANS 6:3–10 (MOMS' VERSION)

Let us not forget, even for one moment, that we are ministers with full-time jobs. Our ministry as mothers is a 24/7 affair. There is no PTO, no sick days available for us. Our ministry is continuous, and it is deeply, eternally important. We work in a spiritual life-and-death situation.

We mediate disagreements, all the while ministering the love and grace of God to our kids. We wipe snotty noses and dirty bottoms, all while teaching watchful little ones how to care for others. We organize life, keep a (somewhat) clean living environment, provide meals ~~seventeen~~ three times a day, and constantly launder clothing. Our work is often unseen and unappreciated, but we are nonetheless teaching our children what it means to serve through the example of how we serve our own families.

Moms don't get degrees in motherhood, and there is no special class we can take that will make us more skilled as parents. Instead, we must immerse ourselves in the Word, pore over our families in prayer and, most importantly, keep our ministries to our families in focus.

My prayer is that God would constantly remind us as moms that our daily routines and the ins and outs of regular life are anything but routine or regular. Instead, they are a ground that is fertile for seeds of life to be planted, for great ministry to take place, and for beautiful fruit to be borne in due time. Because, if we're honest, isn't that what it's really all about?

Perseverance reaps a godly reward in due time, I do believe, and we should settle for nothing less for ourselves. Let's be a generation of moms who are in it to win it!

Also, there is no greater satisfaction than that which comes from knowing that one day, our children will ~~have~~ to get to take care of US, clean up OUR messes, and change OUR diapers...and we will be way less cute as geriatrics than they were as babies.

They best get their Billy Graham on by then.

STUFF MY KIDS SAY

*When leaving swim lessons and
saying goodbye to her teachers:
"Thank you, Ms. Julie. I don't like you, Ms. Maureen."*

—Emerson Watts, age 3

XIII

Chick-Fil-A (Again)

*"Ma'am, we're gonna need you to
never come back here again, okay?"*

—Every Chick-fil-A employee alive

Before I share this story with you, I would like to offer one disclaimer: this story has no, nada, zero, zip, zilch spiritual application. I'm not even going to try to find one, so just take it for what it is—a story about a terrible, horrible, no good, very bad day that will definitely give you some perspective when you think your day can't get any worse.

Now, let's start with some good news and some bad news.

The good news? Well, I haven't—technically—been banned from Chick-fil-A.

Yet.

I do predict, however, that it is only a matter of time before I am served a restraining order by the East Lake Chick-fil-A in Marietta, Georgia. And honestly, I wouldn't blame them. Not even a little.

The bad news? I will spend the remainder of my years fighting a full-on anxiety attack every time I darken the doors of my favorite fried chicken establishment.

Before I delve into the harrowing details of my story, I want to take a second to chase a rabbit, of sorts. I want to say something to all of those mothers who sit in Chick-fil-A with their perfectly behaved little children who are eating their perfectly healthy grilled nuggets and their perfectly portioned fruit cups (because we all know that perfect children don't eat fries): I hate you. No, seriously. I. Hate. You.

See, I'm the mom over in the corner. The one who's worn and haggard and looks ten years older than she is. The one who's yelling at her kid because he's hiding his chicken nuggets down his pants by his...er...nuggets. My kids are the ones crying because their fries are gone and they don't want their FRIED chicken nuggets; they want more of the greasy, starchy goodness that is the waffle fry. It's my kids who are wailing and gnashing their teeth simply because they aren't allowed to trade their ~~stupid~~ educational Chick-fil-A books in for ice cream unless they eat a dang chicken nugget. It's not a French-fry restaurant. It's a chicken restaurant. It's not called "Fry-fil-A," is it? So eat your daggum nuggets.

I digress.

I would be remiss if I didn't take a moment to remind you that I have what one might call a "history" with this restaurant. The East Lake Chick-fil-A, specifically. See Chapter Four if you've forgotten (but I doubt you have).

About a year and a half after the dust had settled from the first fiasco, we were in our favorite haunt again when my son suddenly became ill and explosively vomited all over me and lots of other stuff/people/food.

In hindsight, I wonder why I ever thought it was a good idea to return to the East Lake Chick-fil-A (or any Chick-fil-A, for that matter). But the chicken is just so good...

I guess I thought the worst was behind me. So I let my guard down. I settled in. I grew complacent; I was too trusting, probably. I thought I had this "taking kids out to eat" thing down to a science.

I didn't.

The day I'm going to tell you about started well enough. That morning, I scooped up my youngest son and drove to pick up my dear friend's kiddos because she had recently broken her foot. Being the awesome person with the non-broken foot that I was, I took her kids for the day and brought them to my house. We baked cookies. We cooked spaghetti sauce. We played. Then I had a bright idea.

"Self," I thought, "you should really take the kids to eat lunch somewhere to get them out of the house and give them some playtime. Somewhere like…[wait for it]…CHICK-FIL-A!"

I piled everyone in the car and drove to the infamous Chick. It was smooth sailing. Lunches ordered: check. Lunches eaten: check. Ice creams ordered: check. Ice creams eaten: check.

Commence to playtime in the play place.

A good friend of mine was with me, and we started talking. At this point, I thought I had it in the bag. Everyone had even gone to the bathroom, and the kids were playing well together. About five minutes into my conversation with my friend, though, two of the three kids ran out and told me they needed to go to the bathroom. I left the other kid, the one who will henceforth be referred to as The Perpetrator, playing with my friend's son while I took the other two to the potty. They took care of business and quickly returned to the playground, while I settled back into a chat with my friend. During this time, I'm pretty sure she made the comment, "Hey, isn't it awesome? None of your people have peed or thrown up at Chick-fil-A today!"

Wow.

#CanYouSayForeshadowing?

About five minutes later, a Chick-fil-A employee walked up and interrupted us.

"Ma'am, is that your boy in the bathroom?"

I stared at him, confused. I glanced at the playground, where I saw my son and my friend's daughter playing well together.

"No," I told the man. "All of my kids are on the playground."

"You're sure your boy's not in the restroom?"

"Yes, I think I'm pretty positive," I told him as he walked away.

And I was pretty positive. That's the same as almost positive. Meaning not quite positive. Still, something didn't sit right with me, so I got up and went into the play area. I called each of the kids:

Foster? Check.

Pippi? Check.

Jake? Crickets. JAKE? Crickets.

At this point I realized, to my dismay, that my broken-footed friend's youngest son, The Perpetrator, was NOT in the play area, and that he was in fact, very probably, in the restroom.

I ran to the back of the store and found a teenage employee standing outside the men's room. It was about that time that I heard the screaming. The screaming I must have been ignoring because MY kids were on the playground, and if there's screaming that is not coming from MY kids, then I just tune it out.

Now I heard it loud and clear.

I quickly deduced that during the time a few minutes earlier that I was taking the two kids to the toilet in the women's bathroom, The Perpetrator must have stealthily snuck out of the play place and gone into the men's restroom. We were like ships passing in the night, and nary the two shall meet, or however that goes.

I looked at the Chick-fil-A employee and told him I needed to go into the men's restroom. He nodded his head.

I opened the door.

People, there is nothing on God's green earth that could have prepared me for what I was about to see/smell.

When I opened the bathroom door, this is what I saw:

The Perpetrator (age 3), naked, covered in poop. His clothes in a pile, covered in poop. The toilet, covered in poop. The urinal, covered in poop. And the restroom floor. Covered. COVERED. In. Poop.

Diarrhea, actually.

And the smell. Oh, that smell.

I threw up in my mouth. Now before you go accusing me of exaggeration, let me state, for the record, that I ACTUALLY threw up IN MY MOUTH. I have heard many people say that before, and I am pretty sure that it actually happened zero of those times.

It happened this time.

The stench singed hairs in my nose I didn't even know I had.

Now, to a normal person, this situation would have been overwhelming. Frustrating, Terrifying.

I, however, am not a normal person. I do not have a normal history with Chick-fil-A. The irony of this situation did not escape me, and so I did the only thing that seemed natural to me.

I laughed. Like, REALLY laughed. Hysterically. Tears-pouring-down-my-face, couldn't-talk-couldn't-breathe kind of laughing. Screaming laughing. So hard that I was sobbing because I couldn't get it together.

All the while, The Perpetrator was standing, naked, staring up at me, telling me that he was dirty and needed me to clean him up.

HAHAHAHAHAHAHAHAHA!!!!!!!!!!

I didn't know where to start with the mess. He had "tried" to clean up the bathroom himself, succeeding only in rubbing orange poop into the white grout with toilet paper that had disintegrated into a million tiny fibers on the bathroom floor. He had "tried" unsuccessfully to get on the potty, thus smearing orange poop all over it. He had even "tried" to sit in the urinal, leaving butt-smudges of poop everywhere.

Everywhere.

I was at a loss. I was laughing uncontrollably.

I finally stepped back outside, where the teenage kid was still standing. I needed cleaning supplies (obviously). The problem was, I couldn't tell him what I needed because I couldn't talk. I couldn't stop laughing/sobbing. I tried to tell him, and I even tried to explain myself, laughing/sobbing out something like, "I know it's weird that I'm laughing when this kid has had explosive diarrhea all over the men's bathroom, but you have to understand my history."

Because that made sense. That fixed it. Right...

Finally, I was able to make him understand what had gone down and that I needed cleaning supplies—stat. He went off to look for a mop and bleach. And air freshener. And anti-bacterial wipes. And, well, you get the idea.

About that time, a man walked up to the bathroom. I told him in no uncertain terms that he could not, SHOULD NOT, go in. I directed him to the ladies' bathroom. He looked irritated and huffed off.

I went back in the men's restroom, barely able to see through the laughter-tears. The employee came back, this time bringing his lucky friend and the store manager, who at this point probably has my face on a wanted poster hanging in his restaurant.

I heard things like, "Oh, it's not that bad," and, "Oh, we've seen worse," and, "You know, this happens more than you might think."

And I knew it was all lies.

I refused to let them clean it up. I just couldn't. Instead I, the crazy lady, got on my hands and knees and scrubbed the bathroom from top to bottom, maniacally laughing the entire time I did it. With a naked, poopy kid standing at my side.

After what felt like twenty minutes had passed, I was finally done. With the bathroom, that is. Now it was time to tackle the poop-covered Perpetrator standing next to me. The manager left, commenting on just how fresh the bathroom smelled. I am 99% sure it still smelled like rotting flesh and that, by that point, we were just immune to the odor.

Anyway, I took The Perpetrator and put him in the sink. I started washing and scrubbing. I doused him in antibacterial soap and hand sanitizer, and then I cleaned some more. By now, it was just the teenage employee and me left in the men's restroom, along with The Perpetrator, of course.

As I continued to wash the poop from every crevice on his body, the bathroom door swung open. A middle-aged man walked in. He looked at me.

Now, one would think this was a shocking sight, not something one sees every time one walks into the men's room at a fast-food joint: a teenage boy, a woman, and a three-year-old kid being bathed in the sink.

Apparently, though, this guy must see it all the time.

He walked in and glanced at me, nodded his head, then walked to the urinal directly next to the sink I was using to bathe The Perpetrator. He stared straight ahead, unfazed, unzipped his fly, and whipped out his fire hose. The next thing I heard was the steady stream of tinkle in the urinal.

It was at this point that I officially lost my mind. You would think it would have already happened, but I had managed to hold onto just a shred of sanity. However, when brother-man whipped out his junk and started the evacuation process twelve inches from me like it was just another day in the men's room, I couldn't stop myself. I stared at him in awe, threw my arms up in the air and yelled, "Well...OKAY, THEN!"

I fell on the ground in a ball, laughing until I thought my head was going to explode. I looked up when I heard him finish, watched him shake off (yes, literally, he shook off), zip up his drawers, and walk out the door (the sink was currently occupied by the poop-covered kid bathing in it, so I can't fault him for skipping the hand washing).

The teenage Chick-fil-A employee had eyes as wide as saucers, and I was coming unraveled. I grabbed The Perpetrator from the sink and carried him out into the restaurant, naked, along with the industrial-size garbage bag full of soiled 3T clothing, and went to gather the other two kids.

I realized then that practically everyone in the restaurant had to have heard the commotion (i.e., my hysteria) coming from the bathroom when I saw that every eye was trained on me as I walked out. Well, they were either on me or on the still-slightly-poop-covered naked kid I was holding.

I somehow managed to get the other two kids in hand and we walked out of the restaurant together, me laughing/screeching/crying all the way to the car.

This is real life. This is my life.

And this is the part where I normally add some spiritual wisdom, some Scripture, some truth for us to hang our hats on. I'm not even going to try, folks. As Jeff Probst says to the losing team on *Survivor* week after week, "Sorry. I've got nothing for ya."

The only thing I can think to leave you with is simply this:

LIFE IS FUNNY.
LIFE IS HARD.
EITHER WAY, LAUGH OFTEN.

STUFF MY KIDS SAY

"Mommy, you're my really best.
And Daddy, you're just a little bit the most."

—*Emerson Watts, age 4 (obviously already displaying*
excellent judgment)

XIV

Contentment

*"Too many people spend money they haven't earned to buy
things they don't want to impress people they don't like"*

—*Will Rogers*

I hate commercials. Like, loathe them.

I used to think they were cute, funny even. I'd watch things like *The
Super Bowl* and *The Oscars* just to see what hilarious ads marketing execs
had come up with to make me want to buy something I didn't need.

I'd tear up at the Publix Christmas commercials. You know the ones
I'm talking about: a mom is baking Christmas cookies with her two children when through the door walks Daddy, who is in his fatigues and is
single-handedly making a Christmas wish for his safe return from war a
bona fide Christmas miracle.

Then there's the elderly widow who is alone for Christmas, so all the
neighbors pitch in and decorate her house and invite her to Christmas dinner so she doesn't have to spend Christmas alone. All was right in the world
for the minute and four seconds that the commercial ran, and everyone
who saw it had a case of the warm fuzzies.

Then I had kids.

I can honestly say that nothing irks me more (well, maybe a few things
irk me more, but let's go with this for emphasis' sake) than when commercials come on during my kids' TV time.

Now, I know you don't let your kids watch any TV; I also know they probably spend most of their time exploring the great outdoors, collecting bugs and leaves and eating bark. Or maybe they are in Kiddie CrossFit and are getting their cardio on. Perhaps you are raising the world's next Steve-Jobs-creative-genius, and your little inventor just can't get enough of building circuits and blowing things up.

I want to go ahead and be up front with you, though: my kids watch TV.

Not all the time; they can play outside with the best of them when ~~I lock them out~~ the weather is nice. But I'd say, for transparency's sake, they watch at least two shows per day (please, no one tell Michelle Obama).

Now that I've gotten that taken care of, let's get back to the topic at hand: commercials. In my house, it always happens around the same time. It's 6:45 a.m., and my kids are up like little alarm clocks without a snooze button. They get their ~~water~~ juice and settle in to watch a show while I make breakfast. *Power Rangers* is their current favorite. I can always tell when the first commercial break hits because of the increase in crowd noise in my home. My kids, who moments before were sitting so quietly on the couch, imagining themselves morphing into dinosaur-robots and samurai warriors just like their Power Ranger friends, sit up straight and lock their eyes on the TV. They start talking amongst themselves excitedly. Then they yell. Then they foam at the mouth.

"MOMMY!"

Oh. No.

"MOMMY, you HAVE to come see this RIGHT NOW! Quick, it's gonna go AWAY! MOMMY! Come HERE! RIGHT NOW! MOMMYMOMMYMOMMYMOMMYMOMMY!"

I walk around the corner from the kitchen. "Yes, honey, what is it?"

"MOMMY, it's a STUFFIE! I want one of those for my BIRTHDAY! MOM, I NEED ONE 'cause it has SEVEN pockets that keep my TREASURES safe! STUFFIES, mom, it's what's INSIDE that COUNTS! PUHLEASSSSEEEEEEE? Can I HAVE one?"

Did I mention that her birthday is ten months away?

After trying to explain that, unfortunately, we are not going to be able to call that phone number "up there" and "buy some money to pay for one," as my daughter so wonderfully put it one day, I head back into the kitchen to finish mixing up the pancake batter. Seven minutes later, commercial break number two hits.

"MOMMMMMMMMMMMM!"

Breathe. "Yes, son?"

"FLIPEEZ! It's the SUPER FUN action hat that comes alive right before your EYES! MOM, I NEED ONE! You squeeze the puff ball in the tassel and FLIP, FLIP, FLIP YOUR FLIPEEZ!"

Sigh.

"MOMMY! It's a SEAT PET! I REALLY WANT ONE! They make trips more fun to take, and my seatbelt will always be secure! My head won't dangle anymore, and I'll never ask you again if we're 'there yet!'"

Thank you, my As-Seen-On-TV friends, for nothing.

After explaining to my children that not purchasing a Stuffie is no cause for weeping and moaning and utter misery and that it's really more of a "first-world problem" for a kid to have, I go back into the kitchen, to my happy place, away from the infomercials that suck my kids in, product by product, enticing them to spend money on more junk they don't need.

It's easy to get onto my kiddos, to correct them as situations like these arise. It's easy to say, "Be thankful for what you have," and, "Don't know you know there are starving kids in Africa?" It's easy to be pious, to be the one who, in front of my kids, practices an attitude of thankfulness and contentment.

Then I get alone.

I want stuff. I want trivial, stupid, wasteful stuff I don't need. I am not content. I am rarely satisfied.

Are you?

Maybe it's material stuff. Like, I really, really want a pair of Hunter rain boots—not because they're any better than other rain boots, but because they're Hunters. I want some Lucchese cowgirl boots, too, you know, for all that cowgirl stuff I do.

I want a new minivan. Let me say, first of all, that yes, I do realize that I wrote "minivan," and yes, I do realize that this officially removes me from the categories of all things cool. However, just being transparent, I want a new minivan. A pimped-out Odyssey or Sienna with a DVD system (for my TV-watching kids) and leather seats and a cool navigation system (even though I rarely get lost).

Maybe it's not material things that lure you away from contentment. For instance, I really want a hot body like _____. After three kids, even the skin on my kneecaps is sagging, my hips are large and in charge, and I'm not content with how I look. I very easily fall into the sin of coveting the way others look physically. I want a magic infomercial to offer me a product to "fix me," for appearance's sake.

Maybe you want the life that other women appear to lead, the wonderful husband that _____ gushes on and on about, or the world's most well-behaved children just like _____ (feel free to insert my name here). Maybe you want to be "more spiritual" and sought-after for advice like _____. Maybe you still desire, like you did when you were twelve, to be part of the "in" group.

Whatever your struggle might be, know that not one of us can avoid waging this battle between discontentment and being fully satisfied in Christ. It's a war that will rage until the day we're perfected in Christ, and let me tell you, I can't wait for that day! It's exhausting, this battling with our flesh and sinfulness, isn't it?

The Bible calls this attitude and condition of the heart, very simply, *coveting*.

COVET: To yearn to possess or have _____; to desire, crave, have one's heart set on, hunger or thirst for.

Having stuff isn't bad. We all have to have material things, emotional health, and physical health to survive. The shift to coveting, however, takes place when we remove the Lord from the throne of our hearts and instead place _____ there. When we yearn to possess _____ more than we yearn for Him. When we have our hearts set on _____ rather than on Him. When we hunger or thirst for _____ instead of hungering and thirsting for the Spirit of God and the Word of God.

> *Do not lay up for yourselves treasures on earth, where moth and rust destroy and where thieves break in and steal, but lay up for yourselves treasures in heaven, where neither moth nor rust destroys and where thieves do not break in and steal. For where your treasure is, there your heart will be also.*

MATTHEW 6:19–21 (ESV)

> *Whoever is greedy for unjust gain troubles his own household.*

PROVERBS 15:27A (ESV)

> *For what will it profit a man if he gains the whole world and forfeits his soul?*

MATTHEW 16:26A (ESV)

> *Do not love the world or the things in the world. If anyone loves the world, the love of the Father is not in him.*

1 JOHN 2:15 (ESV)

No matter the area of our discontentment, we have to remind ourselves of the basic truth that we have everything we need in Christ Jesus; after that, it's all just gravy.

Truthfully, most of our discontentment is deeply rooted in what pastor Andy Stanley refers to as "RPP," Rich People Problems. By the way, chances are good that, if you're reading this book and sitting somewhere with a roof over your head while you do so, you are rich by the world's standards. You might not feel rich. You might shop with coupons or drive an old beat-up minivan with a crack in the windshield. You might have a "fluffy" body that's not as chiseled as you'd prefer it to be. You might think you deserve a man who's more in tune with your needs, more helpful, more loving.

But.

For the most part, we are dealing with RPP.

#RichPeopleProblems

Can I tell you something ugly about my true self right now? Sometimes, when I'm weak and vulnerable and worn down, I pity myself. It's disgusting.

It's disgusting because there are things in this world, actual things, that deserve our pity. Things like poverty. Not poverty as in "I'm at the end of my budget month and I can't afford a nice meal out." Poverty as in "I live in a home made of mud and newspapers, and my belly is distended because I haven't eaten a proper meal in days."

Things like war and genocide. Things like the Syrian refugee crisis, which is being called the worst humanitarian disaster since WWII. Things like women and children being killed and mutilated in Africa, all in the name of a vacant god who isn't going to come through for them in the end.

Does this make you uncomfortable?

It should.

It makes me uncomfortable, and it makes me feel ashamed. Ashamed for all of the times when I have complained over my lot in life, over my middle-class dream-of-an-existence.

We hear ourselves saying things like, "We don't really have any room in our budget to cut back on anything," or, "Gosh, I wish I could make something good for dinner, but my grocery budget is gone for the month, so we have to make do with mac and cheese and frozen veggies." Oh, the horror. My kids ate GMOs at each of their THREE MEALS today. God forbid.

We complain about our "wrecked" bodies, saying our kids did this to us and now we're paying for it, when there are women who are aching, literally ACHING, to be able to wreck their bodies so they can become mothers.

We complain that the spark is gone in our marriages while we have men who love and cherish us and are committed to their families and while single moms and victims of domestic violence would do anything to have a "regular" marriage.

I am sick of myself. I am sick of this mindset. I am sick of this culture. I am sick.

Many of the poverty-stricken people are sick, too. They're sick physically and materially. But they're more often than not rich in spirit.

How is this possible?

Because money is an idol and an obstacle, and it keeps us, more often than not, from experiencing God and experiencing joy. There, I said it.

We see money as the solution to all of our problems when, in fact, money is usually at the ROOT of all of our problems.

Some days, I get so angry at my own sinfulness and selfishness that I just want to run to a third-world country to experience the joy that those people have IN SPITE of their situations.

Please hear my heart when I say this: sometimes I am jealous of them.

There's a story in the Bible, specifically in the book of Matthew, about a rich young man who has everything he will ever need materially. He comes to Jesus and asks Him how he can have eternal life. Jesus tells him to keep the commandments, and the young man, probably feeling very relieved, says, "Oh, I've done that." He then asks Jesus what else he lacks, and Jesus tells him, simply, to sell all of his possessions and follow Him. The Bible says the young man went away sorrowful, because he had some fabulous possessions that he just couldn't get rid of. After he leaves, Jesus tells His disciples:

> *Jesus told his disciples, "Do you have any idea how difficult it is for the rich to enter God's kingdom? Let me tell you, it's easier to gallop a camel through a needle's eye than for the rich to enter God's kingdom."*

MATTHEW 19:24 (MSG)

What a terrifying, life-altering, important statement Jesus made in this moment! It's as though Jesus knew that money and stuff would become our ball and chain; imagine that!

I have been thinking about this a lot lately, about what it means to sell everything and follow Him. This might not mean I must literally sell everything I have...but maybe it does. The point is that it's worth considering.

I don't have a fancy conclusion chapter or some step-by-step action plan ready to engage. I am still in process. I am still sifting through my thoughts.

But something has to change in my heart, in my home, and in the homes of those belonging to the global Church.

We've got it all backward.

Contentment comes not from having everything we want or even everything we need, but from keeping an eternal perspective on our possessions, our hearts, our bodies, and our spirits. We will never have "enough" to meet the desires of our flesh. But we always, always have enough in Him.

My prayer is that, when we stray into the alluring land of discontentment, the magnitude of the beauty and majesty of our wonderful God will quickly draw us back to Him.

Every. Single. Time.

STUFF MY KIDS SAY

*"Mommy, I got a baby in my belly today.
I poo-pooed real hard and then it just climbed
right into my tummy. Isn't that neat?"*

—Emerson Watts, age 3

XV

Worn

"I am old, Gandalf. I don't look it, but I am beginning to feel it in my heart of hearts. Well-preserved, indeed! Why, I feel all thin, sort of stretched, if you know what I mean: like butter that has been scraped over too much bread. That can't be right. I need a change, or something."[iv]

—J.R.R. TOLKIEN, *The Lord of the Rings*

Don't Bother Cleaning Your Carpets

It has been a crazy day here in the Watts house. Yes, as I write this chapter, I am no longer sitting on the Lido deck of a cruise ship; I have assimilated back into real life (and summer vacation, at that), but not without my fair share of culture shock! Have my kids always talked this loudly?

The part of me that cares about my reputation as a mother would like to write about our hour of family prayer time this morning, our bread-baking extravaganza this afternoon, followed by my children washing each other's feet, as all servant-hearted siblings do.

Yeah, it went something like that.

In reality, I feel like I have been playing referee all day long, focusing my energy on keeping little people with more energy than NHL hockey players from beating the snot out of each other at a moment's notice.

"You took my cracker!" BODY SLAM!

"He said he loves Daddy more than I do!" UPPER CUT TO THE CHIN!

"She acted like she was going to touch my boo-boo!" TKO!

There is no doubt about it: I am already tired again. I have aged quickly. I have wrinkles on my wrinkles and cellulite on my elbows. I already need another vacation. You probably do, too. All of us deal with the same stresses, the same workloads, the same feelings of fatigue and impatience and anxiety. I know we all struggle with wanting to be good moms and not damage our children beyond repair (even though they severely damage us).

The good FAR outweighs the bad, but I am mentally and emotionally scarred in ways from which I will never fully recover, and I have walked through experiences with my children that bring me to the ledge. That ledge where I feel like if they push me one more time, I'm going over. I'm embracing crazy. Lock me up and throw away the key, because Prozac ain't gonna be strong enough anymore.

One such experience happened almost exactly five years ago. I remember that because it was right before my youngest child was born; I also remember that because it is forever etched in the recesses of my mind.

It was a hot morning in May. Actually, it wasn't that hot until my blood boiled and smoke came out of my ears.

It was a Thursday morning like any other. I was getting my two big kids ready for preschool, running around getting breakfast made and teeth brushed and all of the other chores that seem to recur day after day after day. I was eight months pregnant with Foster, my third child, and believe you me when I say that I was as big as a house. He was my third child in as many years, and my body didn't know up from down (well actually, that's not true; gravity had done quite a work on parts of me that I didn't even know could sag, so I guess it just didn't know UP).

It was around 8:00 a.m., and we had already been going strong for a couple of hours. My then three-year-old daughter and I had gone back and forth and around and back again about her attire for school that day. Let's just say, to keep it short and sweet, that she has opinions about clothes. A lot of opinions. To this day, I typically allow her to pick her own stuff, because what do I care if she is wearing stripes and polka dots and plaid and Disney Princess cowgirl boots all at the same time? She does her thing and she makes it work.

On this particular day, though, I had chosen her school clothes because it was field day and her teachers had requested shorts, shirts, and tennis shoes. Trying to respect their request, I laid out her outfit and explained to her that, just for this day, I was going to make the decision about her attire. This did not go over well with my ~~stubborn mule~~ opinionated angel, who commenced to argue throughout the morning for her right to wear her Easter dress and her ballet shoes.

On the other hand, I had my son, who at almost two was fully in the throes of mischief and exploration. He was the happiest little sinner you could find, a regular comedian, and he was always into something.

After finally getting the kids dressed and prepared for school, I headed to my bathroom to throw myself together as quickly as possible (and by that I mean I wiped yesterday's smudged mascara from under my eyes and threw concealer on a wicked-huge zit that had surfaced). I began to brush my teeth while eyeing the clock and giving myself a mental ten-minute countdown to get all of us out the door. While I was brushing, my daughter walked in. Naked.

"Um, Emerson, where are your clothes?"

"What clothes?"

"The clothes we just put on you for school, along with that French braid that you requested and have now pulled out."

She just stared at me. I asked her again. She stared. Then she said, simply, "I don't want to wear them."

Oh, well, that explained it.

I was irritated, but I kept my cool as I calmly told her that it would be in her best interest to go and redress herself in a very timely manner. She, of course, burst into tears, and as we all do whenever we don't get what we want, she threw her naked self on the floor in a fit of rage.

As she was crying, my son walked in. He had taken his clothes off, as well. And he was covered in poop. Like, poop-caked-between-his-fingers-and-toes covered.

At this point, a couple of things went through my mind simultaneously: 1) "I think I am gonna ralph," seeing as I was eight months pregnant and had a VERY weak stomach, and 2) "Oh, no, the carpet!"

When we purchased our home, the carpets were worn. Honestly, that's putting it mildly. I think I referred to them as "germ-infested." A more apt term would be "janky." Just janky. Upon moving in, I had wanted to have them cleaned since we were not in a place financially to have them replaced right away, but I decided to wait until closer to when the baby was due so that I could feel semi-okay about laying him down on the floors without worrying that he was going to get e-coli or something.

Well, I finally got them cleaned…the day before my son walked into my bathroom covered in poop.

#Sigh

I did what any good mother would do in that moment: I held my breath, grabbed my son, threw him in the shower, and turned on the water. Now he was screaming because the water was cold. My daughter was lying in the floor of my room, screaming over her wardrobe. And, because I picked up my son to put him in the shower, I was now coated in a layer of poop all down the front of my new maternity blouse.

I made sure my son was okay in the shower, stepped over my flailing daughter, and walked tentatively into the rest of the house. I was terrified to see the carpets.

I walked down the hallway toward the first room with carpet, the room where I had left my son playing. It took everything in me not to cry when I walked through the doorway and found his clothing, his nasty, dirty diaper, and poop footprints all over the floor. It looked like an invisible little poop monster had come and run laps around the carpet.

With a sinking heart, I walked to the next carpeted room to find the same thing. And the next. And the next. That little rascal had managed to step in enough poop to track it good and heavy through every single carpeted room in the house. The day after the carpets had been profession-ally cleaned. While my daughter was throwing the world's worst temper tantrum. While I was eight months pregnant and as big as a house.

I went back to the bathroom and showered my son while trying to keep my breakfast down. At this point, he was playing joyfully in the shower. Fabulous. I decided to leave him in there to play while I dealt with my seemingly PMS-ing three-year-old daughter.

She actually beat me to it. As I turned around to speak with her, she walked up to me and took my hand. What she said is forever etched in my memory as some of the most amazing words ever spoken by the world's most precocious child.

"Mom, I know you're frustrated right now, and I get it. But this [she paused here, motioning to the clothing I had once again laid out for her to wear] is NOT working."

Oh. My. Wow.

At that point, I couldn't decide whether to laugh or cry or just lie down and take a nap. I waited for a moment, then I turned and looked at her with my serious-as-a-heart-attack face.

"Emerson. Make. It. Work."

Amazingly, that was the last of the conversation. In that moment, she realized that the mommy monster was about to emerge from hibernation, and she knew better than to provoke me. She frantically put on her clothing as I peeled off my poop-covered shirt, still makeup-less and even farther from being ready than I had been ten minutes earlier. We were officially late for school. Obviously.

I threw on some sweat pants and a t-shirt, dressed Sutton, and flew out the door to school. I figured that since he had already ground the poop into the carpet with his *Chariots of Fire*-inspired sprints, it wouldn't hurt for it to sit until I got home to start the cleanup process.

Which I did. I scrubbed and I scrubbed. And scrubbed some more.

You could still see every footprint stain until the joyous day we ripped up the carpets and installed hardwoods throughout the house.

As cheesy as it sounds, some days I wish I had kept a remnant of that janky, poopy carpet. Because when I think about it, I remember the chaos that I am capable of handling. I remember that even when I feel like I'm at my breaking point, I'm really not. I remember that tomorrow is a new day. I remember how much I have grown as a mother since then, and I laugh so hard every time I think of that story. Because even though it was a disaster, we made it through fairly unscathed.

As mom, we juggle a lot of balls. Or, maybe more appropriately, we juggle a lot of poop. Even when the crises are not life-threatening, even when we're not dealing with earth-shattering issues, even when we are trying to help our daughters through clothing dilemmas and attitude problems, we are often covered up in D-R-A-M-A. And we often feel overwhelmed.

I love what the Lord promises us in Isaiah 40 (MSG). He assures us that even when we are exhausted and worn, He will never fail us, and He will refuel us to fight another day for those we love:

> *God doesn't come and go. God lasts.*
> *He's Creator of all you can see or imagine.*
> *He doesn't get tired out, doesn't pause to catch his breath.*
> *And he knows everything, inside and out.*
> *He energizes those who get tired, gives fresh strength to*
> *dropouts. For even young people tire and drop out,*
> *young folk in their prime stumble and fall.*
> *But those who wait upon God get fresh strength.*
> *They spread their wings and soar like eagles. They run and*
> *don't get tired, they walk and don't lag behind.*

That's quite a promise. It's something we can cling to on our best and our worst days. We are weak, but thankfully He is strong. He is so strong that I can't even wrap my brain around it. And in His strength, He holds us near. I don't know about you, but I sure am grateful!

I'm also grateful that, before we tore up the carpets, I had them cleaned again about a year later. The following day, my youngest threw up his spaghetti dinner all over the carpet in the playroom.

Twice.

Que sera, sera.

STUFF MY KIDS SAY

"Mom, what if you had a porcupine baby? It would hurt your mouth SO bad when it came out. I bet it would take your tonsils out, just like mine!"

—My apparently clueless son, Sutton, age 6

XVI

Fruit

Blessed are all who fear the Lord, who walk in His ways.
You will eat the fruit of your labor;
blessings and prosperity will be yours.

—Psalm 128:1–2

Do you remember being seven years old?

Unfortunately, due to Polaroid film, I am forced to remember this era of my own childhood regularly.

I had an overbite the size of Texas, and my curly mane was wild and untamed. I should have been a child model. I wanted desperately to audition for Disney's *The Mickey Mouse Club*. Can you picture it? Me, Britney, and Christina, all vying for the attention of a certain Mr. Ryan Gosling. He would have picked me, obviously. I ~~blame~~ credit my mother, Lindsay, for helping me blossom into the stunning seven-year-old beauty queen I was.

When I was seven, my best friend, Heather, and I would get together to play hamsters. That's right; while some kids played house or Barbies, we (the homeschoolers) played HAMSTERS. We were each hamsters, and we shared a cage. We built nests on the floor to sleep in and rigged baby bottles to hang off the wall upside down so we could lick the nipples to get water, just like a hamster does from her water bottle. We lay pretend hamster babies and raised them into fine, world-changing hamster adults.

We were fantastic.

I give you this background to help you understand that I wasn't always the fine specimen that I am today, and also to explain why the following story made me giggle/weep.

My daughter is now eight. She is wonderful and fabulous and sweet and funny. She is so, so much cooler than I was at seven. She has beautiful golden-brown hair that is shiny and smooth and has the perfect amount of natural body. She has a great attitude, and she helps me around the house. She loves art and dolls. She does not have headgear (yet), and she has never, not EVER, played hamsters or licked bottle nipples (praise the Lord)!

However, she is still eight.

When she comes home from school each day, I get an earful from her about all that went on—the good, the bad, and the drama. Most days, she's peppy and upbeat, loving life and school and her friends.

Then there are the hard days. I remember one such day several months ago.

Emerson arrived home from school, and I immediately noticed that she was a little down. After helping her unload her backpack and get a snack, the following conversation ensued.

Me: Are you okay, Em? You seem a little bummed this afternoon.

Em: (SIGH) I'm okay.

Me: Are you sure? Because I can usually tell when you're sad, and you seem sad.

Em: (SIGH) Well, I guess I'm a little sad.

Me: What's wrong, baby?

Em: Mom, you know that girl in my class, the one who is always mean to me? Well, today on the playground she started a band. It's called "The Turtle Rockers" [pause to stifle the laughter], and she asked all of my friends to be in it, but she told me that I can't join. And I don't care about being in her dumb band, but I wanted to play with my friends and they wouldn't play with me because she told them that if they were going to be in The Turtle Rockers, they had to stay with her and practice and not play with me. My own friends wouldn't even let me come over to the monkey bars because that was their band room, and I'm not in the band. [Cue the waterworks.]

Me: Ummm...they   named   themselves   The   TURTLE
ROCKERS???

Em: Huh?

Before you become alarmed, this was not the end of our conversation, and of course, I kicked myself because the first question I asked was a snarky response to a seven-year-old's terrible choice of a band name. However, can we all agree that "The Turtle Rockers" is just awful? It sounds like a band that Zack Morris might have played in at Bayside High's senior prom. Am I right or am I right?

Back to the intentional parenting moment.

After fighting back laughter, I gathered myself and dove into a difficult conversation with Emerson. It's not like this was the first time she was left out or hurt by a friend, but I think that, for some reason, this time it especially hurt.

See, this girl in her class really seemed to find satisfaction in being the mean queen bee of the first grade (which does blow my mind). I didn't realize mean girls start that young. All year long, she made it a priority to tell Emerson that she was not her friend, and she even resorted to calling her names and making fun of her outfits in front of the class. ("Oh, look who's wearing overalls...what is it, FARMER day?")

Now, don't get me wrong. I'm sure Emerson has had moments of unkindness herself, and I'm not by any means saying she is without faults. I do know, however, that this situation proved to be hurtful many times over, and that my daughter just couldn't wrap her brain around why the founder and lead singer of The Turtle Rockers would enjoy treating her so unkindly.

After a lot of listening, I challenged Em with this thought: to join the mean girls is to become a mean girl, and you are not a mean girl. Therefore, you might just have to stand alone.

There are always going to be mean girls. There are always going to be "cool" cliques. And sometimes, many times, you'll yearn to be a part of that crowd. However, if being "cool" means you mistreat others and represent your Heavenly Father poorly, it's just not worth it. Period.

We talked about why she is at her school and what it means to stand alone and dare to be different, even when it's isolating. We talked about seeking out the lonely and the hurting and about being the hands and feet of Jesus to them, even if it's by doing something as simple as asking them to walk on the track together during recess. We talked about not engaging hatefulness but, instead, with kindness and humility, operating out of a heart of love—no matter how awful someone is behaving.

These are hard discussions. Hard, but necessary.

And as I thought and prayed about her situation last night, it occurred to me that, as a 30-something woman, not much has changed since my own seven-year-old days ~~in the hamster nest~~ on the playground. There are still mean girls; they have just learned how to make fun of you more subtly. There are still the "cool" cliques, and they are still selective about those with whom they associate. And sometimes, if I'm being honest, I still yearn to be a part of their group. Sometimes, I desperately want to be a Turtle Rocker.

In some ways, it's even harder to navigate these relationships as an adult, don't you think? The pressure we put on ourselves is tremendous. I mean, at this point, we know not to join forces with the mean girls, but a teensy part of us wishes that we were that put together and organized and fit and stylish. And we know it doesn't matter if we're ever classified as "cool," but a tiny part of us still wants to be.

It's bound to happen; we are going to be tempted to join them because we feel like can't beat them. My prayer for those of us who are hidden in Him is this: that we would snap back to reality and realize we're totally, completely focused on...you got it...OURSELVES!

In being so self-consumed, we somehow, so easily, forget the very purpose of our very existence as followers of Christ. To love other people to Jesus by seeking out the lonely and the hurting by being the hands and feet of the Savior to them, which is the very nature of the gospel.

If we have style and swag but don't represent the Savior well, we've missed it. If we have lots of friends but we never step outside our inner circle to engage a broken and hurting world, befriending and walking alongside people who don't look or act or think like us, we've missed it.

Don't miss it.

I love, L-O-V-E how The Message interprets Romans 12:9–21:

> *Love from the center of who you are; don't fake it. Run for*
> *dear life from evil; hold on for dear life to good. Be good*
> *friends who love deeply; practice playing second fiddle...*
>
> *Bless your enemies; no cursing under your breath. Laugh*
> *with your happy friends when they're happy; share tears when*
> *they're down. Get along with each other; don't be stuck-up.*
> *Make friends with nobodies; don't be the great somebody.*
>
> *Don't hit back; discover beauty in everyone. If you've got it in*
> *you, get along with everybody. Don't insist on getting even;*
> *that's not for you to do.*
> *"I'll do the judging," says God. "I'll take care of it."*
>
> *...If you see your enemy hungry, go buy that person lunch, or*
> *if he's thirsty, get him a drink. Your generosity will surprise*

him with goodness. Don't let evil get the best of you; get the
best of evil by doing good.

Do you know my favorite line in that section of Scripture? "Make friends with nobodies; don't be the great somebody."

Lord, give us eyes to see the lonely and the broken, and give us feet that run to them. Give us hands that serve the needy and hearts that love the hard to love. Humble us, and instill deep within us the truth that we ourselves are lonely and broken and needy and hard to love. And remind us that because You chose to love us in spite of us, we also should choose to love others.

In the face of weighty decisions about what we're willing to sacrifice in order to be accepted, we would do well to follow my daughter's lead. You see, her story didn't end with the parental pep talk. Thankfully, it ended in action.

Fast-forward about six weeks. A lot happened in those six weeks. Several days after our talk, Emerson was actually permitted to join The Turtle Rockers. She was stoked. They met on the playground every afternoon during recess and "wrote songs." She was accepted into the fold, and she was loving life; she was no longer the outcast.

As the days progressed, however, Emerson began to notice that the Queen-Bee-Turtle-Rocker leader was alienating other girls in the class, and while Emerson was experiencing life as a cool kid, many of her friends were not. She realized that even though she wasn't personally being rejected anymore, others were, and it bothered her. She approached the Queen Bee several times and tried to talk to her, asking her to be kind to everyone and to allow anyone interested to join The Turtle Rockers. She came home each day more and more bothered, and I did my best to remain silent and let God work in Em's heart. I listened when she talked and simply prayed that she'd be bold and courageous for Christ.

My husband and I went out of town for ten days, and I felt pretty out of the loop. So as soon as I arrived back home, I sat down with her and asked her about how life had gone while I was traveling. She told me about her spelling test and about her softball game and about her loose tooth. Then I casually asked her how things were going with The Turtle Rockers.

"Well, Mom," she said, "I actually quit The Turtle Rockers last week while you were gone."

Wait what? I was temped to erupt into cheers and applause, but I maintained my cool-as-a-cucumber façade as she kept talking.

"I just got tired of seeing kids in my class get their feelings hurt because they were left out. I started to worry that, because I was in The Turtle Rockers, they might think that I was a mean girl. And I'm not a mean girl, Mom. So I told Queen Bee that I quit, and now I play with lots of kids on the playground at recess instead."

Oh, my heart. She got it. And she got it on her own. I didn't have to nag at her or tell her what to do. I simply engaged in conversations with her about real-life situations, presented her with truth, and then let the Holy Spirit do the rest of the work in her heart.

This is the fruit of motherhood. It comes when we least expect it—often, actually, when we least believe fruit will ever grow. Then it does, and it's beautiful and revitalizing and humbling.

God really doesn't need our help; I think He just lets us help so we get to be a part of His ministry in the hearts and lives of His people. He doesn't owe us fruit, but He graciously gives it to us anyway, perhaps as gentle reminders that our work as parents is not in vain.

Thank you, Lord.

Ironically, a few weeks later, higher powers at the school shut down The Turtle Rockers for good. Why? Because they were being hateful to other kids and it was becoming a big issue within the classroom. I, for one, wasn't sad to hear the news.

#TheTurtlesAintRockingNoMo

STUFF MY FRIENDS' KIDS SAY

"Mommy, look what I found!
These tiny, tickly, tasty pellets!"

—*My friend's five-year-old daughter, referencing her*
newly discovered chest

XVII

Eternity

"What we do in life echoes in eternity."

—Maximus Decimus Meridius, *Gladiator*

Doctor Love

There was a period in my life when most of my disposable time and income were spent at the pediatrician's office. Maybe yours were/are, too.

Before I make my children sound like complete germ-infested monsters, let me explain. All of my precious children have had their own health challenges. My firstborn dealt with chronic ear infections and severe constipation (just getting the inevitable poop reference out of the way early). My middle child dealt with everything from salmonella poisoning as an infant (must've been all that sushi I was feeding him) and terrible acid reflux to chronic ear infections and a bad attitude (that one can't be cured by visiting the pediatrician—just figured I'd lump it in there with the rest of his issues). My third one took the cake, though, when it came to doctor's visits. From an eye infection that landed us in the emergency room when he was ten days old and an infantile fever at seven weeks that earned us a four-day admittance to the local children's hospital to severe reflux, a milk protein allergy, constipation, chronic ear infections, and ultimately ear tubes, he has been one expensive gift from God.

Yes, I guess I just made them sound like complete germ-infested monsters.

And no, I don't need your dietary suggestions, and no, we're not going gluten-and-dairy free. More power to you if that's your bag, but it just ain't gonna happen on this shift.

And yes, they take vitamins and eat lots of vegetables and fruits, and they even take Juice Plus+.

And no, I really don't want your holistic practitioner's phone number.

Anyway, back to the pediatrician.

Over the last decade, I have gotten to know our office staff, the nurses, and our doctor ~~way too~~ well. They have seen me laugh. They have seen me cry. They have laughed with me. They have shared Starbucks with me because, for a while there, I was too busy for friends—and really, who needs friends when you have nurses—so I just stopped and picked them up some coffee every time I was on my way in. Also, I am 98% sure they snuck me back to a room faster because of it. Or maybe it was because my kids terrorized the "sick" room.

#WhateverWorks

Taking your kids to the pediatrician is no small feat, am I right? I'd show up, rush to get in on time, and dish out yet ANOTHER copay. The receptionist would cheerfully ask me to sign the credit card slip, and I'd bite my tongue to keep from asking her if she just wanted to go ahead and set up a direct deposit from my paycheck into the doctor's bank account to cut out the middle~~wo~~man.

I usually found myself presented with a dilemma once I finished the check-in process. I'd have one kid that was sick and two that weren't (or, should I say, weren't sick YET). So I'd send said sick child into the "sick" room and said well children into the "well" room. Then I'd go back and forth, watching like a hawk to make sure my children didn't cross the threshold into the other room, either contaminating or being contaminated. I would often find my children lying on the carpet in these rooms, because why would they want to stand or sit like normal people when they are in the single-most-germ-infested place under the sun? Last time I was there, I found my four-year-old lying on his stomach underneath some chairs, sucking goldfish crumbs off the carpet. Not. Kidding. I went ahead and penciled in a sick visit for him three days later in order to treat whatever bacteria he had just sucked off the floor.

Once my nurse, my boo, Jo, called us back to our room, my kids would stop at the scale and beg for a lollypop. You know which kind—the same ones pediatricians were giving out thirty years ago when we were kids. The Saf-T-Pop.

There's nothing new under the sun, is there?

Just for the record, Saf-T-Pops are not SAF. Those suckers (pun intended) come off the Saf-T stick so fast that sticks might as well not even be included with them. They should just call them Chok-Ing-Pops.

When we'd finally get to our room in the back, which is about 3' x 3' (for four people plus a doctor) and includes zero toys, one of my children would inevitably drop his Saf-T-Pop on the ground. At this point, one of three things typically happened: 1) I'd grab it and trash it and get that child a new one, 2) it fell and shattered into a million pieces and I "got to" clean it up and THEN get him a new one, or 3) said child was faster than me, grabbing it before I could get to him and popping it back into his mouth, at which point I would schedule a sick appointment for three days later (see the goldfish example above).

At this point, my kids were usually bouncing off the walls and in tears because "he touched me." Add to this the inevitable, "Are we done yet?" and "I need to go potty." By the time the pediatrician made her way in to see us, it appeared that I was a mother who could control neither her children nor herself and that all four of us quite possibly needed to be medicated.

While I would try to speak to the doctor with some semblance of intelligence, the non-sick kids tended to do things like grab the tongue depressors and medical gloves or knock her costs-thousands-of-dollars otoscope off of the exam table. Or maybe one might come back from the bathroom carrying a full cup of urine because she "wanted to tinkle in a cup." Not that it's ever happened to me.

We would finally prepare to leave, and I would have the pleasure of trying to herd my crew out of the room, assist them in making their sticker selections (which can take hours, for reals), pick up any prescriptions, and get back down to the van in the parking garage with the help of the world's slowest elevator.

I need a nap just remembering those days.

I must tell you that I am beyond thankful for my pediatrician. She has been a part of the healing process of my children's lives; she has hugged me when I was overwhelmed; she has taken each and every situation affecting my children's health and well-being on a case-by-case basis, knowing them by name and not just as another number. She knows their bodies. She knows my parenting style. She has cared for my children well, and I am so very grateful.

We invest a lot into our children's physical health, as we should, because they're worth it.

So what about investing in their spiritual health?

Do I minister love to my children's hearts and attend to their spiritual health as much as I do their physical well-being? Am I as in tune with their emotional ups and downs as I am with their coughs and sneezes? Do I labor over what I allow to penetrate their minds and spirits through media, friends, and environments as much as I do over what I allow to nourish (or not) their bodies?

Physical health is so important, but spiritual health has eternal implications.

Do I give my children state-of-the-heart checkups?

Do I give them to myself?

Test yourselves and find out if you really are true to your faith. If you pass the test, you will discover that Christ is living in you.

2 CORINTHIANS 13:5A (CEV)

Examining the state of our physical health can mean the difference between life and death. Examining the state of our spiritual health can mean the difference between eternal life and eternal death.

Do we create time to be still, to sit before the Lord and seek His guidance and His equipping as we attempt to raise little humans—not just into functional adults but, more importantly, into passionate pursuers of Jesus Christ?

Here are some simple questions we might ask ourselves as we get really honest about our successes and failures as mothers:

1. Do I prioritize spending time in communion with God, creating the personal time and space to do so?
2. Do I pray for my children? Often?
3. Do I speak words of life and love into my children daily, even when it's not easy?
4. Do I live authentically before my children, sharing with them my own depravity and desperate need for Jesus and confessing when I have behaved sinfully (when appropriate)?
5. Do I discipline and guide my children by dealing with root heart issues and not just surface-level symptoms?
6. Do I live and breathe God's Word as I communicate with my children, showing them that Scripture is meant to be part of the fabric of who we are as Christ-followers?
7. Do I exemplify a child of God who is desperately in love with her Heavenly Father, a living example of what is means to have relationship with God, instead of being someone who just follows a religion?
8. Do I extend the grace of God to my children, the same grace He has extended to me time and again?

There are, most definitely, many more questions we can ask ourselves. Maybe, though, asking ourselves these questions would be a good place to start. Maybe in the asking we will open ourselves up to the Spirit's prompting to dig deeper, to ask more questions.

I want to say one thing to all my sisters out there (because I know how we women are, how we can operate in the impossible realm of perfectionism): asking these questions and realizing we come up short is NOT grounds for taking a battering ram to our hearts and beating ourselves to a bloody pulp. Crushing our own confidence and breaking our own spirits completely contradicts what asking these questions should actually do for us. None of us will answer every question with a "yes," and most of us will find that we fail often. These questions, and our answers and shortcomings, should not stir up fear or apprehension in us, because our questions are rooted in a deep love for the Lord and for our children. And in love, there is no fear or anxiety.

> *There is no fear in love, but perfect love casts out fear. For fear has to do with punishment, and whoever fears has not been perfected in love. We love because he first loved us.*

> 1 JOHN 4:18–19

Will you join me in this self-examination? Will you come before the Lord without pretense, laying every piece of yourself before Him so that He can refine your heart to more like the heart of Christ? Be forewarned, this process can be uncomfortable. Sometimes God takes a wrecking ball to our hearts because they desperately need to be broken. What He then rebuilds, though, is worth the pain and is more beautiful than we could have fathomed. When our hearts become aligned with the heart of the Father, we are in a much better position to administer God's love to our children.

Moms, we are doing Kingdom work. What we're doing has eternal impact.

God, give us eyes to see motherhood in light of eternity.

Here's to being moms who are unwilling to settle for mediocrity when the ultimate satisfaction and fulfillment and equipping has been offered to us by our Father.

Here's to being moms who want to love our children to the cross.

Here's to being moms who are committed to making our own walks with the Lord a priority, because we know that when we are spiritually healthy, we are more capable to doctor love to our children.

And here's to all the pediatricians out there. Dr. Mekelburg, I may have paid enough copays to fund your vacation home, but I have to say that you deserve it. For all the times you have been pooped on, I say bravo. For all the times you have been exposed to some disgusting stomach bug that manifested itself in you the next day at 1:00 a.m., I say soldier on. For that time a few weeks ago when my son kicked you in the face, I say sorry. Just sorry.

Legos and Life

It's 8:15 in the morning, and while I'm in the middle of ~~watching HGTV and eating bon-bons~~ washing the never-ending supply of dirty dishes left for me in the sink, I hear the shriek. You know the sound: the one that escapes a child's mouth and reverberates off the walls of the house for several seconds. The high-pitched, someone-just-gouged-out-my-eyeballs scream.

I drop what I'm doing and run, soapy hands and all, to my six-year-old son's bedroom, prepared for the worst. I round the corner to find him purple-faced in the middle of his floor, about to pass out from holding his breath for twenty seconds. I run to him and gather him in my arms. I check for blood and teeth fragments (hey, it happens), and when I don't find anything amiss, I try to talk to him.

"Son, what happened? Breathe, baby, and tell Mommy what happened!"

I can't decipher any human language through the blubbering, snotty, hot mess that is my son, so I ask him again.

"What happened, buddy? Answer me!"

This time I gather a bit more information.

"Fooosssstttteeeerrrr something-something-something WAAAAH HHHH!"

Using my best mommy-detective skills, I insightfully gather that my youngest son, Foster, was involved in this tragedy. I call him into the room.

He enters, wide-eyed and angelic, the "what, me?" look plastered on his face.

After everyone (i.e., my spastic son) has calmed down, I ask one final time, "Boys, what in the world happened in here?"

Sutton, still upset, manages to finally get it out: "Foster picked up my Lego spaceship and broke the rocket boosters into pieces!"

Oh. My. Gosh. All of that drama over Legos. That can be put back together. That are MADE to be taken apart and put back together.

It takes everything in me not to chastise my son for scaring the you-know-what out of me by reacting like he was being disemboweled. I hold my tongue and hug him for a moment, then I correct the offending party and ask him not to break his brother's Lego space shuttle again. Then back to the dishes I go.

Legos are kind of Sutton's thing. He has ten million of them, and he is forever building airplanes and cars, rockets and castles. He has a ginormous Lego table with a huge drawer to store the ten million pieces.

In theory.

Ironically, more often than not, I find Legos everywhere BUT his Lego table. In the washing machine. In my printer. Inside the travel-size shampoo bottle. The garbage disposal, the driveway, the bathtub, even in his sister's fish tank. And yes, these are all actual places where I have found Legos.

Nothing brings me closer to losing my religion than stepping on one of those little torture devices. If I really wanted to feel that much pain, I could just go down to the garage, get a nail, and jam it into the arch of my foot.

Ultimately, I put up with the mess, the screaming, the arguing over who made the best Lego version of Daddy, and more, all because my son loves his creations. They are his masterpieces, and he loves to build. He builds me Lego flowers. He builds for our affirmation. I want to encourage him to build, to be creative, to work hard when he has a vision for something.

What are we building?

I have been studying the book of Haggai (yes, you read that right). If you're anything like me, I kind of thought Haggai was a big snooze fest, an opportunity to let my eyes gloss over and my mind wander. It's a book full of "the word of the Lord came by Haggai," and "on the twenty-fourth day of the sixth month in the second year of Darius the king," and "Zerubbabel son of Shealtiel." Even the prophet's name, "Haggai," sounds sort of dweeby. Yes, I know it's in God's Word and is therefore important, but I'm just being honest when I say that, in the past, I liked to breeze over that book of the Old Testament.

I recently, however, decided to dig into Haggai to see what I could learn. And learn, I did! Here's a synopsis of what happened during the time of Haggai the prophet:

After many, many years in Babylonian captivity, God called the Jews to return to Israel to rebuild the temple that had been destroyed. Only a remnant of the people obeyed, and upon returning, they realized that building the temple was going to be hard. It was a big job, and the workers were few.

So instead of obeying God, the Jews put off the temple project and instead focused on building their own homes and families and lives, even going so far as to say, "The time has not come...for the house of the Lord to be rebuilt." Which was untrue, because God had clearly shown them that it was, indeed, the right time. He wanted the temple built for His pleasure and His glory—He does not like to share the spotlight, and rightfully so.

So in order to gain their attention, God allowed a drought in their land. The drought affected their food sources, their animals, and even the people themselves. God used Haggai to help the people see the error of their ways, and the people ultimately obeyed God and began to build the temple. As a result, they experienced God's presence and His glory as He poured out blessings on them for walking in obedience.

I took in the history and chewed on this for a while. And then I prayed and asked God to show me how this related to me, today, right now. And I believe He spoke.

You see, all of us as women and as moms are building something. We are always building. Some of us are building careers, others families. Some are building stock portfolios and others social status. Maybe we are even building our physical images.

Building is not a bad thing, right? But the question is this: who are we building for?

I believe God is calling you and me to lay down our own building plans, exchanging them for the blueprints drawn up by the ultimate Architect. I believe He is asking us to build something of far greater value than the things of this world, to build something that magnifies His glory and not our own.

Is there something to which you sense God calling you? Maybe He's been nudging you for a long time now.

"Build my temple."

It's hard. It takes time. Maybe the job seems impossible, too big to take on. Maybe it's overwhelming and you're tired, and maybe tackling the kind of building project He's calling you to oversee seems extremely daunting.

"Build my temple."

Israel's temple was the place where God's glory was illuminated. What is God calling you to "build" to shine His glory far and wide? Are we so distracted by building for our own temporal gain, like the Jews who returned to their country from Babylon, that we have forgotten the eternal things to which God has called us?

> *Then the word of the Lord came by the hand of Haggai the prophet, "Is it a time for you yourselves to dwell in your paneled houses, while this house lies in ruins? Now, therefore, thus says the Lord of hosts: 'Consider your ways. You have sown much, and harvested little. You eat, but you never have enough; you drink, but you never have your fill. You clothe*

*yourselves, but no one is warm. And he who earns wages does
so to put them into a bag with holes.' Thus says the Lord of
hosts: 'Consider your ways. Go up to the hills and bring wood
and build the house, that I may take pleasure in it and that
I may be glorified,' says the Lord. 'You looked for much, and
behold, it came to little. And when you brought it home, I
blew it away. Why?' declares the Lord of hosts. 'Because of my
house that lies in ruins, while each of you busies himself with
his own house.'"*

HAGGAI 1:3–9 (ESV)

Are we so concerned with our own "buildings," like my son and his Lego space shuttle, that they have become everything to us? If so, we must repent. We must lay down our earthly tools and exchange them for the ever-abundant tools of heaven.

Oh, that we wouldn't miss what He has for us! Not because we need to "do" more for Him, but because, like my little one and his Legos, the joy is in the building when we're building for HIM. And our Heavenly Father gives us the chance to be a part of His story, a part of things that last and matter—eternal things.

Kind of like Legos. They last.

Last time I checked, Legos were not biodegradable. They are the gift that keeps on giving, probably for centuries to come. I find another one every day, usually with my foot, and in those moments I curse the world's Legos and beg the Lord to end my misery and beam me home to Him.

Bride of Chuck E.

No, not the Child's Play Chucky doll with the head that rotates 360 degrees. He's Creepy McCreeperson.

I'm referring, of course, to Chuck E., the largest, friendliest, most birthday-loving rodent in all the land. Chuck E. Cheese.

I try to avoid Chuck E. when at all possible, mainly due to the complete assault on my senses that occurs the moment I walk in the door of his headquarters.

Of course, my children love Chuck E. Cheese's. L-O-V-E. I am pretty sure that when they picture heaven, it looks an awful lot like The Chuckster's pad, complete with mother-of-pearl Skee-Ball machines, diamond-encrusted slot machines, and a 24-carat gold ball pit.

I am also pretty sure that when I picture hell, I see it resembling a non-air-conditioned version of the same thing.

Up until a couple of years ago, Chuck E. Cheese's was but a distant, fond memory from my childhood. I am pretty sure my eighth birthday party was celebrated with The Chuckster, and I am pretty sure it was the greatest day of my life. I still remember how their cheese pizza was made with a sauce that had tiny diced tomatoes in it and that I was allowed to have root beer to drink. I remember the anticipation that would build in my gut during the moments leading up to the Chuck E. Cheese's stage show which, in my mind, ranked right up there with the Country Bear Jamboree at Disney World. It was a magical, magical place.

Or so I remembered.

It's a funny thing, time. It has a way of painting beautiful pictures of events that, in all actuality, were terrible in every single way.

This seems to be the case with Chuck E. Cheese's.

My first adult encounter with The Chuck-man took place about two years ago. I took my children to a birthday party there. On a Saturday.

If you're a parent, you just shuddered.

At first, I was so excited. Overcome with a major sense of nostalgia, even. I built this day up for my children, preparing them for what was to be the best moment of their brief little lives. The games. The tickets. The prizes. The miniature Ferris wheel. The Skee-Ball machines—oh, those Skee-Ball machines! My kids could hardly sleep the night before. And let's face it, neither could I.

We drove up to this little piece of heaven and anxiously made our way inside, where a wall of noise like nothing I'd ever heard before hit my ears like a sledgehammer.

The frequencies that pierced my eardrums were borderline painful. High screams, low screams, wails, shrieks of excitement. I felt a bit disoriented, like maybe I had accidentally walked into the wrong place, a place that resembled Dante's seventh level of hell.

As we were herded like cattle through the railed walkway, we pushed and shoved our way to the entrance gate, where one of Chuck E.'s happy helpers stood ready to stamp our hands. You see, at Chuck E. Cheese's, security is of the highest priority; therefore, they make sure to stamp parents' and children's hands with matching numbers so that, upon exiting, the adolescent security force can confirm that adults are, in fact, leaving with their own children and not someone else's. Which is pretty funny, if you think about it, because after an hour in that place, every adult would be so sonically and experientially scarred by what had just gone down that most parents probably try the opposite thing and attempt to sneak out alone for the sake of some blessed peace and quiet.

Anyway, we made it to the gate, and the pubescent happy helper boy stamped my hand with the number 16. He stamped my daughter's hand with the number 16. I sent her through the gate and turned around to find my son. After locating him (he was drinking from another child's sippy cup), I grabbed him and pulled him to the gate to get his hand stamped. The happy helper stamped his hand. With the number 19.

Huh?

"You must be mistaken," I told him. "You stamped me with the number 16. You just made him a 19."

"Oh, that's close enough," said the boy.

Okay, can we pause here for a second? I know that our schools are not what they used to be (sorry, teacher friends, but we all know it's true), but seriously? "Close enough?"

Choosing between the value of my time spent attempting to explain basic math concepts to the boy and my concern for "security," I opted to just go with it, nod my head, and enter Dante's Inferno.

The next two hours were a blur of activity. Trying to get my children to participate in the birthday party at hand while the sights and sounds of Chuck E. Cheese's beckoned to them. Trying to keep my eyes on my children at all times while they ran in opposite directions, worried that my son would be joining the family of number 19, never to be seen again. Taking potty breaks every five minutes because their bladders were loaded with red-dye-number-40 fruit punch. Apologizing profusely because my daughter pushed open the emergency exit door and set off the site-wide alarm. Twice.

The noise. The people. The smells. The tickets. The tokens.

The ticket redemption.

Oh, the ticket redemption process. There's really not anything more frustrating, is there? First of all, any parent worth his or her salt knows that you only give little kids a couple of choices, at most. Otherwise, decision-making becomes the most laborious, stressful process under the sun.

My daughter had 89 tickets. At Chuck-E-Cheese's, 89 tickets could mean anything. Nine toys from the ten-point bin, or three toys from the 25-point bin, or one toy from the 50-point bin plus one toy from the 25-point bin, or two toys from the 25-point bin plus four toys from the ten-point bin, or...you get the idea.

But even this wasn't really the problem. The problem was that she wanted the 50,000,000-point bag of cotton candy up on the top shelf. Top shelf items aren't for sissies...they are for Skee-Ball champions. Which I was pretty sure my seven-year-old was not. And so we ended up leaving with two packs of Smarties, one temporary tattoo, one sticky hand, and one gorgeous "diamond" ring. And tears, because we were cotton candy-less.

#Sigh

Honestly, I'd be okay with never setting foot in that place again. Unfortunately, my kids beg—BEG—to go there. If they are working toward a special outing, if he is trying to earn a treat for five nights of dry Pull-Ups, if she's attempting to get a reward for reading ten books on her own, what they usually want to do is go to Chuck E.'s. Even though, at the end of it all, they usually leave disappointed and in tears. And cotton candy-less.

I am a lot like my kids. I have grand ideas of what will bring me happiness and fulfillment. I live in a world of "if only's." *If only I can do _____, I will be so happy. If only I can get _____, I'll be content.* But the truth is, I'm never satisfied.

And we are all this way. Do you know why?

Because we were made for more than this life can offer us. We were made for more than Smarties...we were made for the cotton candy. The problem is, we live in a Smarties world.

However, if we know and trust Christ, we have an amazing promise of hope. We have the promise of cotton candy from the Master Candy-Spinner Himself.

This might seem like a stretch of a tie-in, but go with me here.

In the same way that Chuck E. Cheese's is heaven on earth for my children, I have my own activities and things and trips and you-name-its that I look to for happiness and fulfillment. *If I can just make it until my vacation*, I think, *then I'll be relaxed and happy.* And the vacation is all well and good, but then it's back to reality and I face disappointment. I anticipate the day I can buy _____, and once I get it, I feel let down, because I realize that there is a void in me that no object can fill.

Don't get me wrong—there's nothing wrong with THINGS. There's nothing wrong with vacations or leisure activities. These are all well and good. But they don't—they won't—they can't fulfill us.

Because we were made for more.

When you're made for heaven, even a weeklong trip to the British Virgin Islands is a little bit of a disappointment, know what I mean?

When you're made for cotton candy, Smarties are a bit of a letdown.

I am the bride of Christ, not the bride of Chuck E. Nothing else is going to satisfy me like Him, either here on earth or in eternity. And I know that once I see Him face to face, once I enter life as it should be and not as it is now, I will never lack for anything again. I will be fully satisfied, never disappointed. I will be drowning in cotton candy.

"No eye has seen, no ear has heard, no mind has conceived
what God has prepared for those who love him."

1 CORINTHIANS 2:9

We can't comprehend the ultimate satisfaction He has in store for us. We can only guess about what it will look like, grasping at tiny fragments of fulfillment we experience here on earth.

May we live with the hope of cotton candy, a hope that shines the light of Jesus to those around us.

Lastly, I just want to say that, after being reawakened to the mouse, the myth, the legend that is Chuck E. Cheese's, I am actually 98% sure that I had nightmares as a kid from watching the robotic Chuck E. sing his songs with those demon eyes and motorized ginormous mouse hands. I'm as creeped out by him today as I was when I was eight.

Epilogue

'Cuz It Sounds So Fancy When I Say I Wrote An Epilogue

I have always wanted to write an epilogue. Now that I'm doing it, I actually must say it feels amazing. The final word on my book of words. I feel like Hemingway must have felt after he finished *The Old Man and the Sea*. Wait…let's be real: I've never read *The Old Man and the Sea*. Maybe I feel more like Tina Fey must've felt when she finished *Bossypants*. Yes. Definitely.

My epilogue is simple, ladies. In fact, it can be summed up in four words. Ready

TAKE A CRUISE. ALONE.

For reals, y'all.

You might remember that when I started this book, I was sitting in a cruise ship terminal, preparing to board a five-day cruise all by myself. Well, cruise alone I did, and AMAZING IT WAS!

Maybe you hate boats and the ocean. That's okay (even though it does signal that you're strange and very probably not American). Just GO SOMEWHERE ALONE!

Moms need a break. We need to get away, far from our routines and our kids' needs and our piles of laundry and our minivans. We need time to get reacquainted with ourselves and to relearn exactly who God says we are. We need time to be still and quiet.

As much as I love traveling with my husband (and that's a lot), I found through my cruise experience that time spent completely alone is crucial to my sanity and well-being as a mom.

We need to carve out time in our day-to-day lives, as well, to enjoy our own company. You might find, like I did, that you really like YOU.

Motherhood is serious business that can be full of serious busyness (see what I did there?).

We have to make sure we are filling ourselves up so we can be poured out into the lives of our kids. We have got to find rest. We need community.

We need friends with whom we can be real and vulnerable. We need to carve out time for the things we love to do so that we don't completely lose who we are. Because a haggard, bitter mom ain't fun for anyone.

Motherhood is hard. Anything worth doing is hard. And motherhood is worth doing.

Moms, you can do this.

Just be sure that, even when the going gets hard, you laugh often. Laughter is medicine that never loses its potency.

Feel free to laugh!

--Jordan Baker Watts

Notes

[i] Mark Twain, as quoted on *HappyPublishing.com* (accessed August 25, 2016, https://www.happypublishing.com/blog/early-quotes/

[ii] John Piper, "You Are God's Midwife for the New Birth of Others," *Desiring God. org* (http://www.desiringgod.org/messages/you-are-gods-midwife-for-the-new-birth-of-others), accessed August 25, 2016

[iii] Brooke Fraser, "Hosanna," (Hillsong Publishing, 2008)

[iv] J. R. R. Tolkien, *The Lord of the Rings* (Mariner Books, 50th Anniversary ed. edition, 2005), 32

57610773R10117

Made in the USA
Lexington, KY
19 November 2016